The Gospel Re

The Gospel Revisited

Towards a Pentecostal Theology of Worship and Witness

KENNETH J. ARCHER

✂PICKWICK *Publications* · Eugene, Oregon

THE GOSPEL REVISITED
Towards a Pentecostal Theology of Worship and Witness

Pickwick Publications
An Imprint of Wipf and Stock Publishers
199 W. 8th Ave., Suite 3
Eugene, OR 97401

www.wipfandstock.com

ISBN 13: 978-1-60608-344-4

Cataloging-in-Publication data:

Archer, Kenneth J.

    The gospel revisited : towards a pentecostal theology of worship and witness / Kenneth J. Archer.

    xx + 154 p. ; 23 cm.

    ISBN 13: 978-1-60608-344-4

    1. Pentecostalism. 2. Bible — hermeneutics. 3. Liturgics. I. Title.

BR1644 .A73 2010

Manufactured in the U.S.A.

Dedication

I dedicate this work to the faculty and staff
of the Pentecostal Theological Seminary.

Contents

Permissions

I am appreciative of the following publishers for permission to reprint previously published essays.

Reprinted by permission of Blackwell publishers Inc.

"A Pentecostal Way of Doing Theology: Method and Manner," *International Journal of Systematic Theology* 9 (2007).

Reprinted by permission of Pentecostal Charismatic Theological Inquiry International

"The Spirit and Theological Interpretation: A Pentecostal Strategy," *Cyberjournal for Pentecostal/Charismatic Research* 16 (2007).

Reprinted by permission of Koniklijke Brill N.V.

"Pentecostal Story: The Hermeneutical Filter for the Making of Meaning," *Pneuma: The Journal of the Society for Pentecostal Studies* 26 (2004) 36–59.

"Nourishment for our Journey: The Pentecostal *Via Salutis* and Sacramental Ordinances," *Journal of Pentecostal Theology* 13 (2004) 79–96.

Portions Reprinted by permission of The Pneuma Foundation

"Open View Response to Charismatic Calvinism," *Pneuma Review* 6 (2003) 47–57.

"Open View Theism: Prayer Changes Things," *Pneuma Review* 5 (2002) 32–53.

Acknowledgments

This monograph would not have come together without the tedious work of Brandelan (Sunny) Miller. Thank you for all your diligent work. I am truly indebted to you.

I wish to express my gratitude to The Foundation for Pentecostal Scholarship (www.tffps.org) for their financial support of this project.

Preface

I EMBRACED THE PENTECOSTAL way of life at the age of nineteen and understand my Christian religion as Pentecostal. I am a male of Scot-Irish and English descent, born in the state of Ohio and raised by a hard-working "blue collar" family. I still marvel at the healing grace that the Lord has extended to me over the years. I married a Pentecostal preacher's daughter (a fourth generation Pentecostal who can trace her spiritual lineage back to Aimee Semple McPherson), graduated from a Pentecostal Bible College, and together Melissa and I pastored two Pentecostal churches and one non-charismatic, non-denominational Community Church. I am now in my mid-40's. Since 2002, we have been ministering to the College and Career young adults at Woodward Church of God in Athens, Tennessee. We have raised our sons as Pentecostal Christians and have had the privilege to pray for them and be prayed for by them "at the altar." As Pentecostal parents, we have prayed with them for regeneration, healings, vocational direction, and deliverance. We also have prayed for them to receive the Baptism in the Holy Spirit, and, as I explained to my sons, the initial biblical sign will most likely be tongues as expressed with joyful tears. It is a personal delight that both our sons are actively involved in a local Pentecostal church. They help serve in the community through their participation in worship ministry.

I am grateful for the following individuals and communities for their contributions to my spiritual-theological journey. Foremost, I am thankful for my current Pentecostal Christian community, Woodward Church of God, Athens, TN. I am always amazed at how and through whom the Spirit works in the community. Wade Hockman, an elder in our church, is such a person. His commitment to peace, his prophetic ministry, and personal friendship has impacted me in ways that words cannot express. I will never forget the time I was sitting across from him in a restaurant. I was experiencing an ongoing difficult period in which depression seemed to be my constant companion. With tears in my eyes, I told him that I felt as though I had been in a cold dark winter. Just as I finished that statement, he looked intensely into my eyes, started to physically shake, and with spiritual intensity said, "The Lord has taken you to this place and you will remain in it for some time. Some things can only die in the winter... the Lord is there with you but you cannot see, hear, or sense him. Embrace it, and the Lord will do his work. This is what the Spirit says." Then he sat back in the chair, exhausted. Later that I week I put a screen background up on my computer. It was of a winter scene that was cold and dark, with tress covered in ice . . . an eerie yet beautiful scene. Sometimes the terror of night is not the Devil.

I must say that the essays in this monograph all come out of my teaching experience at Pentecostal Theological Seminary, previously known as Church of God Theological Seminary. I began in 2001. I am grateful to the faculty, staff, and students who have encouraged me in both my teaching and academic writing. During this time I was also privileged to teach courses at the Asian Seminary of Christian Ministry, Philippines; SEMIDUD, Quito, Ecuador; and University of the Caribbean, Puerto Rico. These experiences have broadened my horizon of understanding the beauty, diversity, difficulty, and commonality of Pentecostalism.

The PTS community has contributed to my on-going theological understanding. In particular is Steve Jack Land's *Pentecostal Spirituality*. This has been a source of inspiration and direction for me. My work reflects important ideas he raised in this monograph and offers some further developments. Steve has served as president of Pentecostal Theological Seminary since 2002. In this capacity of President, he has made space for me to work as a theological educator, including academic research and writing. It is risky business to push traditional theological boundaries, but the Vice President for Academics, James Bowers, has helped to shelter me from potential problems and provided needed opportunities to develop my theological vocation.

Steve Land lifted up the importance of the Fivefold Gospel in his first monograph, but Chris Thomas made some significant connections between the Fivefold Gospel and ecclesiastical signs associated with it. I continue to develop that initial paradigm. Rickie Moore and Chris Thomas' work in hermeneutics has also been influential in my own endeavors. Cheryl Bridges Johns' work in formation and ecumenism played an important role in my understanding of the necessity of praxis and a hospitable yet sectarian identity.

I am particularly thankful for my close friends who are also practitioners and theologians. Andrew Hamilton has been a close friend over a number of years. He still answers my phone calls, even at night when I am working through some theological problem. More importantly, he is there when I need someone to talk to and pray with. Terry Johns and Robby Waddell remain sources of encouragement. Another very close friend is Rick Waldrop. He has opened my eyes to the beauty of God's creation through birding. He also has helped me to see the anguish of God's marginalized people, to hear their cries and celebrate in their victories. Rick is more than a friend, he is a confidant.

Lastly, I mention my family because of their importance in my life. Melissa, my wife, sacrifices much for her family including reading through my manuscripts. Her work in biblical studies, ministry, and theological education enriches my life and work in important ways. My sons, Trent and Tyler, inspire me with their music and encourage me with their faith in Jesus Christ.

Introduction

The supreme reality is an overwhelming experience of the presence and power of God in the midst of life. But this captivating of
God is not centered in the announcement of forgiveness of sins
and justification. God is experienced intimately and intensely as
broken lives are reorganized, as those considered 'worthless' and
'insignificant' discover their worth before God, and as those who
thought they could do nothing to change their situation or the
world are empowered to act. This reality is communicated, not by
rational world or doctrinal exposition, but by a ritual of praise and
worship.

—Richard Shaull and Waldo Cesar [1]

Although Pentecostalism can be thought of as traditionalist in its
Christian theology, it differs radically from other Christian group-
ings in placing emphasis on speaking in tongues and its highly
experiential forms of worship, which involve prophesying, healings, and exorcisms. A direct, transforming, personal encounter
with God is seen as a normal feature of the Christian life.

—Alister McGrath [2]

ONE QUIET EVENING AT our home in southeastern Tennessee my
family and I were eating dinner together. As we often do, we were
reviewing the events of the day with each other. Trent, my oldest son,
who was 13 at the time, began telling us about his friend at school. Trent

1. Richard Shaull and Waldo Cesar, *Pentecostalism and the Future of the Christian
Churches: Promises, Limitations, Challenges* (Grand Rapids: Eerdmans, 2000) 146–47.

2. *The Twilight of Atheism: The Rise and fall of Disbelief in the Modern World* (New
York: Doubleday, 2004) 194. McGrath affirms Pentecostalism as an important recovery
of experiential Christianity which may have potential to influence both the religious and
especially atheistic West He states, "it is this form of Protestantism (Pentecostalism) that
may be expected to resist erosion by atheism. Pentecostalism is strongly predisposed
toward the dispossessed and oppressed, undermining one of the most atheistic critiques
of religion—that it oppresses" (215).

explained how they had become friends over the past weeks. While he was telling us all about his friend, I could tell that he was concerned about something. Trent said, "Daddy, he is a Baptist. I told him that we were Pentecostal. Now, just what exactly is a Pentecostal, anyway?"

What is Pentecostalism? Traditionally, this question is answered through careful historical analysis and identification of a distinct doctrine which sets it apart from other groups. A history of the Pentecostals is one helpful way at getting at a definition of Pentecostalism.[3] However, such an endeavor can also be problematic. For example, Alan Anderson, in *An Introduction to Pentecostalism: A Global Charismatic Christianity*, devotes 15 pages to defining Pentecostalism.[4] He is correct to recognize differences between "classical" and "neo" Pentecostalism, as well as charismatic manifestations of Christianity. He argues that "'Pentecostal' is appropriate for describing globally all churches and movements that emphasize the working of the gifts of the Holy Spirit, both phenomenological and on theological grounds—although not without qualification."[5] Furthermore, Anderson will use the term Pentecostalism in a broad sense so as "to include all the different forms of 'spiritual gifts' movements."[6] Anderson's primary stated goal is to challenge the existing presuppositions and paradigms used by white North Americans and western European academic interpretations of Pentecostal and Charismatic history. I do appreciate his concern, especially when historically interpreting "global" Pentecostalism. However, I believe Anderson does not do enough justice in recognizing clear theological distinctions between Pentecostals and Charismatics and theological perspectives that connect the various Pentecostal communi-

---

3. For my definition of Pentecostalism see Kenneth J. Archer, *A Pentecostal Hermeneutic for the Twenty-First Century: Spirit, Scripture and Community* (New York: T. & T. Clark, 2004) chapter 1. Reprinted in paperback as *A Pentecostal Hermeneutic: Spirit, Scripture and Community* (Cleveland, TN: CPT, 2009) 11–46.

4. (Cambridge: Cambridge University Press, 2004, reprinted 2006) 1–15.

5. *An Introduction to Pentecostalism*, 13–14.

6. Ibid., 14. See also his essay "Pentecostalism," in *Global Dictionary of Theology: A Resource for the Worldwide Church*, ed. William A. Dyrness and Veli-Matti Kärkkäinen (Downers Grove, IL: InterVarsity, 2008) 641–48. Anderson states, "The various expressions of Pentecostalism have one common experience and distinctive theme: a personal encounter with the Spirit enabling and empowering people for service, and experience often called the 'baptism in (or with) the Spirit'" (642). I would agree that Spirit baptism is necessary and essential for a Pentecostal theology, but it is not the single indentifying marker. It functions as the linchpin which holds the Pentecostal theology together.

ties.[7] I suggest that it would be better to differentiate between Pentecostal and Charismatic. Pentecostal is a noun which refers to a distinct theological community and theological system.[8] Charismatic is an adjective which modifies an existing theological system without thoroughly transforming it into something new (Calvinism, Lutheranism, Catholic, etc). A Calvinist, for example, would embrace a monergistic understanding of soteriology. Pentecostals are synergistic in their understanding of soteriology. Because of a significant experience of the Spirit, the Calvinist would consider himself/herself as a charismatic Calvinist. From this perspective we affirm a shared common experience in the Spirit, yet remain part of our distinct theological communities. I believe a theological Christian family of Pentecostalism does exist. A Pentecostal theological story generates a certain vision of reality and encourages certain meaningful practices that hold Pentecostalism together as a community. Pentecostalism is an authentic Christian theological tradition.

Paul Alexander's recent publication, *Signs and Wonders: Why Pentecostalism is the World's Fastest Growing Faith,*[9] is an important contribution to understanding Pentecostalism and why it has such popular appeal. Alexander explains the "global" appeal of Pentecostalism in non-technical conversational language that engages the reader through its testimonial sections, humorous reflections, and provocative analogies. In eight chapters, he offers an entertaining account as to why and how Pentecostalism is appealing to people. Each chapter discusses important practices which are generally encountered in Pentecostal churches.

Paul Alexander's proposal as to why Pentecostalism is appealing does not limit itself to one theological distinctive such as the baptism in the Holy Spirit, however that experience might be theologically formulated. Yet, he rightly includes tongues as an important aspect of Pentecostalism. Interestingly, he never offers a definition of Pentecostalism.[10] I suspect that

---

7. Part two of Anderson's monograph does address important theological aspects of Pentecostalism, see 187–286.

8. Of course Pentecostal would also function as an adjective in the case of Pentecostal Christianity.

9. (San Francisco: Jossey-Bass, 2009).

10. He does offer a brief a definition of classical Pentecostalism and Charismatic Christianity. However, this is found in an endnote in chapter three (155 n. 1). A theological definition is not given, just historical, thus baptism in the Holy Spirit with the initial evidence of tongues is not offered as the classical Pentecostal distinctive. In his chapter on tongues speech, the introduction opens with a Baptist's struggle with tongues speech.

the book overall serves as his definition of Pentecostalism, but I believe he has captured important social, theological, and behavioral practices that are significant indicators of Pentecostal theology. As he explains why Pentecostals embrace these significant practices and how such practices reflect Pentecostals' sociological location and theological beliefs, he is indirectly informing the reader's understanding of Pentecostal identity. Alexander points out that Pentecostals have a particular worldview—a more holistic view where miracles happen. They come from a predominantly lower socio-economic location. They tell stories, engage in the joy of expressive worship, and enter into ecstatic experiences. God directs their lives through visions and other "biblically acceptable" means. Pentecostal services are structured improvisation, like jazz. Pentecostals are a hopeful people who love people. This work, which is written for outsiders, accurately identifies key theological practices of Pentecostals. Although Alexander does not express it as such, these practices, I suggest, are held together by a common narrative tradition—a shared Pentecostal story with regional accents, nuances, and particular contributions.

More challenging than defining the historical origins of Pentecostalism is the question concerning Pentecostal theology. Paul Alexander's explanation of Pentecostalism's appeal reinforces the importance that such "theological" communities do indeed exist. Allan Anderson's monograph specifically draws attention to Pentecostals' global existence. Pentecostalism is dynamic and fluid tradition which calls its participants into a particular Christian vision of reality. However, can we really argue that a Pentecostal theology exists? Should it exist? And if it does exist, how is it to be identified? Even though the past decade has seen extensive academic attention given to this subject, the questions concerning Pentecostal identity, theological method, and theology are still contested. I believe that Pentecostal identity is based upon its storied tradition. Furthermore, this Pentecostal storied identity provides the primary context for both a descriptive analysis of a Pentecostal theology and a contemporary constructive Pentecostal theology. This monograph articulates a Pentecostal theology based upon its primary storied identity expressed through its central narrative convictions.

Her understanding of Pentecostals does include the following typical definition, "that salvation was followed by 'baptism in the Holy Spirit' and that this was demonstrated by tongue speaking" (42).

Pentecostalism should be appreciated for what it is—a new living and authentic Christian spirituality with a distinct theological view of reality. In other words, Pentecostalism is a theological tradition even though it is diverse ethnically, geographically, linguistically, economically, theologically, and culturally. Pentecostalism is a diverse group of restoration-revivalistic movements held together by a common doctrinal commitment to the Full Gospel and experiential worship services.[11] The heart of Pentecostal spirituality is the doxological confession pertaining to Jesus Christ and the Holy Spirit, which forms them as a pneumatic-Christological community.

The following essays were brought together into this volume because they all have a common theme—the Fivefold Gospel. The Fivefold Gospel served as the central narrative convictions of the earliest North American Pentecostal communities and can still be heard with some important modifications throughout Pentecostalism globally. The Fivefold Gospel is a formative doxological confession which is testimonial in nature and relational in character. Jesus is the Savior, Sanctifier, Healer, Spirit baptizer, and coming King. Through these central narrative convictions Pentecostals identify themselves as participants in the redemptive mission of the Social Trinity living in the last days. Worship and witness provide the important missional concerns of Pentecostal theology. In the words of Steve Land, "The Spirit of the end groans, sighs and is pressed within in order to drive out toward the world in witness and toward God in worship."[12]

The essays in this volume address various facets of theology via the Gospel. The Gospel should be the heart of any Christian theology and indeed soteriology serves as the story-line of the biblical story. The chapters address Pentecostal method, theology and hermeneutics. Each chapter could stand alone; but, read as a whole, the monograph demonstrates the possibility and vitality of an integrative narrative Pentecostal theology.[13]

11. When using Full Gospel, I am including the Fourfold tradition as well as the Fivefold tradition.

12. Steven J. Land, *Pentecostal Spirituality: A Passion for the Kingdom* (Sheffield, UK: Sheffield Academic, 1993) 192.

13. Chapters 1, 2, 4, 6 were previously published essays. They have some minor revisions and editorial corrections. The rest of the essays are entirely new, except for chapter 5, which is an extensive revision of some previously published materials. The reader will notice some overlap and repetition in the essays, particularly concerning the identification and significance of the Fivefold Gospel.

With this monograph, I do not pretend to offer *the* Pentecostal theology nor attempt a global Pentecostal theology. Mine is an attempt at producing a *local* Pentecostal theology. However, I do believe it will resonate and intersect with other contextualized forms of Pentecostalism located in different parts of the world. It is my sincere prayer that the work will contribute to the ongoing development of constructive contemporary Pentecostal theologies and contribute to the fruitful dialogues amongst the various theological traditions. I pray that the monograph will be a source of blessing for Christians in general and Pentecostals in particular. For those who may not have ventured into the Christian faith, may it provide a warm invitation for you to enter into the redemptive healing power of the Gospel of God. For in the end, Pentecostals will always testify that the living "God is to be experienced and known as a personal, transformative, living reality."[14]

---

14. McGrath, *Twilight of Atheism*, 215.

A Pentecostal Way of Doing Theology

Method and Manner

*The Spirit of the Lord is upon me because he has anointed me to
bring good news to the poor. He has sent me to proclaim release to
the captives and recovery of sight to the blind, to let the oppressed
go free, to proclaim the year of the Lord's favor.*

—Luke 4:18–19

*I am not ashamed of the gospel; it is the power of God for the
salvation of everyone who has faith.*

—Romans 1:16

PENTECOSTALISM AS A CHRISTIAN religious movement has been given much attention by historians, sociologists and even biblical scholars; yet, little attention has been given to the development of a Pentecostal theology. This chapter emphasizes the necessity of doing Pentecostal theology by means of an integrative methodology and in a narrative manner that flows out of Pentecostal identity. Pentecostal theology must move beyond the impasse created by subsuming its identity under the rubric of "Evangelical" in order for it to articulate a vibrant fully orbed mature Pentecostal theology. This can be accomplished only when "Pentecostal" is taken seriously as an authentic Christian tradition with its own view of reality. I argue that one very important way of articulating a Pentecostal theology in keeping with its identity is to ground it pneumatologically and organize it around the Fivefold Gospel.

Pentecostal theology?[1] Often, Pentecostalism is presented as a primitivistic and popularistic revivalistic movement with an apocalyptic forecast for the future.[2] As a religious movement, Pentecostalism has a robust spirituality, but it lacks the intellectual ability and academic sophistication required to produce an acceptable enduring theology.[3] From this perspective, Pentecostalism is presented as a subgroup of popularistic Fundamentalism or at best a conservative group of North American Evangelicalism. Pentecostalism at most may help other Christian communities appreciate the importance of emotive experiential worship services but it really does not offer a distinct theology.

This simplistic reductionism of Pentecostalism is being challenged in various ways. Douglas Jacobsen (a non-Pentecostal) correctly points out that such a "representation of the movement misinterprets both the genius and genesis of Pentecostalism."[4] Pentecostalism should be appreciated for what it is—an authentically new, living Christian spirituality with

1. This essay is a revision of a paper that I presented at the 33rd Annual Meeting of the Society for Pentecostal Studies, March 11–13, 2004, at Marquette University, Milwaukee, Wisconsin. I want to thank the respondents Henry H. Knight III, D. Lyle Dabney and Frank Macchia for their constructive comments. I appreciate the editorial reading of the draft by my colleagues Rickie Moore and Melissa Archer.

2. I realize that there is some validity to these taxonomic tautologies.

3. For one example, see Mark Noll, *The Scandal of the Evangelical Mind* (Grand Rapids: Eerdmans, 1994). For two significant "Pentecostal" responses to Noll's monograph, see James K. A. Smith, "Scandalizing Theology: A Pentecostal Response to Noll's *Scandal*," *Pneuma: The Journal of the Society for Pentecostal Studies* 19 (1997) 225–38 and Cheryl Bridges Johns, "Partners in Scandal: Wesleyan and Pentecostal Scholarship," *Pneuma* 21 (1999) 183–97. See also Amos Yong, "Whither Systematic Theology? A Systematician Chimes in on a Scandalous Conversation," *Pneuma* 21 (1999) 85–93.

4. Douglas Jacobsen, *Thinking in the Spirit: Theologies of the Early Pentecostal Movement* (Bloomington: Indiana University Press, 2003) 355; see further his penetrating analysis of early Pentecostalism's similarities to and differences from Fundamentalism, the Social Gospel, and empiricism (351–64). Jacobsen's work demonstrates that early Pentecostals were contextually situated amongst a range of different theological persuasions. Pentecostalism as a movement was not simply a Hegelian synthesis but was *sui generis*, its own theological tradition (361).

a distinct theological view of reality.[5] In other words, "Pentecostalism is a theological tradition."[6]

Even though there is a growing awareness that Pentecostalism is its own theological tradition, there are some Pentecostal scholars who continue to recast Pentecostal theology into an Evangelical mold. For these, Pentecostalism is an Evangelical tradition first and foremost with the additional distinct doctrine of the Baptism in the Holy Spirit and the initial evidence of speaking in tongues. Thus Pentecostalism is not a separate theological tradition in and of itself but simply an Evangelical movement that has a distinct doctrine—a view that becomes more pronounced after certain Pentecostal denominations became members of the National Association of Evangelicals in the 1940s and 1950s.[7]

One cannot argue for a distinct "Pentecostal" theological tradition if it is really believed that Pentecostalism's roots, soil, and fruit is Evangelicalism, especially the North American version! One would not be able to construct an accurate and explicit Pentecostal theology from the theological and cultural categories that are inherently a part of Protestant

---

5. Richard Shaull and Waldo Cesar, *Pentecostalism and the Future of the Christian Churches: Promises, Limitations, Challenges* (Grand Rapids: Eerdmans, 2000) xiii. For other helpful discussions concerning a distinct "Pentecostal theological tradition" by Pentecostal scholars, see Cross, "The Rich Feast of Theology: Can Pentecostals Bring the Main Course or Only the Relish?" *Journal of Pentecostal Theology* 16 (2000) 27–47; James K. A. Smith, "Advice to Pentecostal Philosophers," *Journal of Pentecostal Theology* 11 (2003); Kenneth J. Archer, "Pentecostal Story: The Hermeneutical Filter for the Making of Meaning," *Pneuma* 26 (2004) 36–59. See also the seminal work by Steven J. Land, *Pentecostal Spirituality: A Passion for the Kingdom* (Sheffield, UK: Sheffield Academic Press, 1993), which argues that Pentecostal spirituality is a distinctly lived experience in the Spirit of God and should be the starting and ongoing contributing aspect of a Pentecostal theology.

6. D. Lyle Dabney, "Saul's Armor: The Problem and Promise of Pentecostal Theology Today," *Pneuma* 23 (2001) 143. Dabney is challenging Pentecostal theologians first to view early Pentecostalism as a spiritually rich tradition with an "implicit theological impulse." Second, he is challenging Pentecostal scholars to develop explicitly a mature Pentecostal theology from the perspective of the third article or pneumatology (141, 144–46). Dabney believes that Pentecostalism is a pneumatologically driven renewal movement that should do theology from the third article of the creed. When Pentecostal Theology is done through the lens of pneumatology, it will become mature theology and will be beneficial to all Christian traditions (145).

7. For example, see John B. Carpenter, "Genuine Pentecostal Traditioning: Rooting Pentecostalism in Its Evangelical Soil: A Reply to Simon Chan," *Asian Journal of Pentecostal Studies* 6 (2003) 303–26.

Evangelicalism. The theological categories are often at odds with the implicit theology of Pentecostalism.[8]

One of the issues that contribute to the debate is the manner in which the origin and emergence of Pentecostalism are understood. The primary focus falls upon the historical antecedents that gave rise to "Pentecostalism." The examination of historical antecedents becomes the means properly to explain the theological matrix of Pentecostalism and then becomes the standard to validate the current production of Pentecostal theology. From this perspective, the definition of Evangelicalism and the contributions of Evangelicalism to Pentecostalism are more of a concern than an understanding of Pentecostalism.[9] One could argue that the world behind Pentecostalism is more important, hermeneutically speaking, than the world of Pentecostalism that generally eclipses the world behind Pentecostalism.[10] No doubt an accurate and fair assessment of the social, cultural, and theological womb that birthed Pentecostalism is important in order to properly understand and assess Pentecostalism.[11] But to sub-

8. Dabney, in his "Saul's Armor," argues that Pentecostals who have theologically assimilated with Protestant Evangelicalism do not have the categories to do Pentecostal theology or worse "have absorbed the false pernicious notion that Pentecostalism is not a theological tradition at all" (121). He says that Pentecostal assimilation into Evangelical identity began in the early 1950s and represents the third stage in North America Pentecostals' struggle with their own identity within the larger Christian communities. For Dabney, Saul's armor represents cultural and theological categories of thinking that do not emerge from the implicit theological impulses of Pentecostalism, thus it needs to be thrown off so that Pentecostals can discover their own voice (115–17).

9. Ian M. Randall, *Evangelical Experiences: A Study in the Spirituality of English Evangelicalism 1918–1939* (Carlisle, UK: Paternoster, 1999). Randall's monograph is an important contribution, yet my concern has to be with his broad definition of Evangelicalism. He follows David Bebbington's definition of Evangelicalism as a movement that comprises all those who share these four common themes: the Bible, the cross, conversion and activism (1, 271). He views Pentecostalism as a conservative evangelical movement because of its view of the authority of the Bible and revivalism, see especially chapter 8, "Old-Time Power: Pentecostal Spirituality," 206–37. In this chapter Randall argues that Wesleyan roots are absent in British Pentecostalism. British Pentecostals "were determined to stake out ground which was identifiably within the central conservative evangelical spirituality" (207–11). It seems that these historiographies want to stress the "immediate" historical antecedent, while minimizing other Christian traditions.

10. The concern for historical antecedent further reinforces my argument that when Pentecostalism entirely embraces Evangelicalism it becomes more modernistic in its theological concerns, albeit modernistic in a theologically conservative way.

11. For an informative read that takes serious the global diversity of Pentecostalism, see Allan Anderson, *An Introduction to Pentecostalism: Global Charismatic Christianity* (Cambridge: Cambridge University Press, 2004).

sume Pentecostalism into the category of Evangelicalism is to exclude aspects of Pentecostalism that are essential to its identity and undermine its capability to present an authentic Pentecostal theology. Pentecostalism is more than the sum total of all the contributing theological antecedents that it embraced, absorbed or rejected, and then transformed into a distinct tradition which has commonalities with most Christian traditions including Evangelicals.[12]

I sense that we more "postmodern" Pentecostal scholars take the "world of Pentecostalism" as our starting-point and, thus, are more willing, post-critically, to appropriate theological insights of other traditions—including those outside of so-called Evangelicalism—into our Pentecostal theological works.[13] Doing Pentecostal theology involves more than simply retrieving and restating or employing a revisionist historiography; it involves faithfully re-visioning our tradition in light of the Spirit and the Word.[14] Thus, what emerges is a mature, Pentecostal, theological articulation of our implicit Pentecostal spirituality.

---

12. See William J. Abraham, *The Coming Great Revival: Recovering the Full Evangelical Tradition* (San Francisco: Harper & Row, 1984) for the problematic nature of the term "evangelical" along with some suggestive resolutions. Abraham argues that there are enough shared characteristics among certain traditions that they can be classified as a family. More important, however, is Abraham's affirmation that those traditions that make up the "evangelical family" must do theology from within their own tradition. This is exactly what I am trying to do and therefore I agree with D. Lyle Dabney that Pentecostals must throw off the evangelical nomenclature and do theology as Pentecostals. See also Donald W. Dayton, "Some Doubts about the Usefulness of the Category 'Evangelical,'" in *The Variety of American Evangelicalism*, eds. Donald W. Dayton and Robert K. Johnston (Downers Grove, IL: InterVarsity, 1991) 245–51, who argues that the category evangelical has lost its usefulness and calls for a "moratorium on the use of the term, in hope that we would be forced to more appropriate and useful categories of analysis" (251). I agree with Dayton. However for a contemporary Wesleyan theologian who is current in this debate and still finds the "evangelical family resemblance" metaphor beneficial in linking distinct movements together, see Henry H. Knight III, *A Future for Truth: Evangelical Theology in a Postmodern World* (Nashville: Abingdon, 1997) especially chapter 1.

13. Some Pentecostals would also want to engage non-Christian religions in dialogue because we believe that the Spirit is working everywhere. For example, see the important work of Amos Yong, *Discerning the Spirit(s): A Pentecostal-Charismatic Contribution to Christian Theology of Religions* (Sheffield: Sheffield Academic Press, 2000) and his *Beyond the Impasse: Towards a Pneumatological Theology of Religions* (Grand Rapids: Baker Academic, 2003).

14. I am purposefully inverting the Protestant approach of Word and Spirit to signal that Pentecostal theology must break from the traditional Protestant paradigm of subordinating pneumatology to Christology. For example, I do not want to follow the

One of the more pressing problems of doing modernistic academic forms of theology is that they become disembodied from community life and spirituality, thus doctrinal statements take precedence over both communal praxis and communal pathos. Orthodoxy, defined as right belief, is the means to explain what is and is not essentially Evangelical. Orthodoxy separated from both orthopraxy and orthopathy becomes a form of cognitive creedalism that, in turn, becomes the means to identify who is and is not "Evangelical." Reference to our specific communities of worship (local churches and denominations) is not as important as affirming the Evangelical creed! Furthermore, who said that all the theological molds have been created? Those Pentecostals who are concerned to be seen as Evangelical first and Pentecostal second seem insistent to argue that current North American Evangelicalism (as though it is some monolithic group) presents the best creedal description of essential orthodox Christianity. At best, Pentecostal "Evangelicals" can argue that Pentecostalism has recovered an additional doctrine but not an essential doctrine. For this group "Pentecostal" is simply an adjective.

Could we not suggest that Pentecostalism is the creation of a distinctly new and, yet, still authentically Christian mold? Rather than arguing that Pentecostalism is Evangelical, should not the greater and more ecumenical concern be to argue that Pentecostalism is an authentic Christian tradition in action and thought? From a grammatical perspective, "Pentecostal" functions both as an adjective and as a noun. It is a distinctly identifiable community embodying its own Christian spirituality. As Terry Cross so aptly stated:

> While Pentecostals share many theological tenets in common with other Christians, we have experienced God in ways others do not confess. Rather than viewing theology as a description of our distinctive, we need to understand the all-encompassing difference which our experience of God makes in every area of our

---

traditional argument that Jesus Christ achieves redemption and the Spirit simply applies redemption, but instead articulate the constitutive and reciprocating missional roles of the Spirit and the Son from a decidedly pneumatological view. I want to avoid the subordination of both the Son to the Spirit and the Spirit to the Son through articulating the missional activity of the Spirit and Jesus in the eschatological transformative redemption of God's creation. For a helpful discussion and proposal to move beyond the traditional Protestant paradigm as it relates specifically to soteriology see Steven M. Studebaker, "Pentecostal Soteriology and Pneumatology," *Journal of Pentecostal Theology* 11 (2003) 248–87.

lives—especially those that are theological . . . Pentecostal theology will reflect the reality of God's encounter with humans, developing the recipe with a special ingredient that flavors the whole dish, not just the relish that complements the main course prepared by someone else.[15]

In re-addressing the legitimacy and viability of doing Pentecostal theology, I will argue that our tradition should express its theology in a way that is faithful to the tradition. The method and manner are organically connected to the body thus affirming a narrative approach that starts from below, among the people who have encountered the Spirit of the living God in community.

I agree with Simon Chan's statement that "the strength of Pentecostal traditioning lies in its powerful narratives." Chan further argues, "Pentecostals have been better at telling their story than explaining it to their children."[16] Chan's statement is revealing. On the one hand, he recognizes the strength of testimony and story as a primary means of Pentecostal traditioning; yet, on the other hand, it appears that this approach is not as helpful because the stories need to be explained. In explaining, Pentecostals may opt for modernistic epistemological modes that are inherently hostile to Pentecostal practices of story-telling and testimony. I believe that part of the problem of "explaining" our theology has been the uncritical adoption of theological methods and forms which contain epistemological and theological perspectives that undermine the Pentecostal spirituality which shaped its story. By employing more modernistic epistemological methods, we undermine the credibility of our spirituality. We rob our narrativity of its formative power, and we become more conservative modernists (academic Neo-Fundamentalists) than Christians of the Spirit and the Word.

The early Pentecostal way of doing theology was expressed by means of testimonies, songs, trances, inspired preaching, and dance. Swiss missiologist Walter Hollenweger notes that early Pentecostals primarily relied upon oral means of communication to express their theology.[17] According

---

15. Cross, "Rich Feast of Theology," 33–34.

16. Simon Chan, *Pentecostal Theology and the Christian Spiritual Tradition* (Sheffield, UK: Sheffield Academic Press, 2000) 20.

17. Hollenweger argues that the narrativity and orality of early Pentecostalism come from the African-American contribution to Pentecostalism. See his "After TwentyYears Research on Pentecostalism," *International Review of Mission* 75:297 (1986) 3–12.

to Hollenweger, the early Pentecostal oral means of communication involved the following:

> orality of liturgy; narrative theology and witness; maximum par-
> ticipation at levels of reflection, prayer, and decision making, and
> therefore a reconciliatory form of community; inclusion of dreams
> and visions into personal and public forms of worship that func-
> tion as a kind of "oral icon" for the individual and the community;
> an understanding of the body-mind relationship that is informed
> by experiences of correspondence between body and mind as, for
> example, in liturgical dance and prayer for the sick.[18]

Hollenweger writes, "the Pentecostal poor are oral, nonconceptual peoples
who are often masters of story. Their religion resembles more of the early
disciples than religion taught in our schools and universities."[19] Obviously,
early Pentecostals were not doing theology in a modern academically
acceptable manner. These marginalized people were doing theology
through narrative forms. Ironically, their way of doing theology was more
consistent with the primary biblical way of presenting theology—through
narrative.

Deborah McCauley's important work only reinforces Hollenweger's
emphasis on the primacy of oral communication and narrative.[20]
McCauley's work addresses an important and often overlooked group in
North American Christianity. She investigates "Mountain Religion"—a
group often overlooked because it is an oral culture.[21] McCauley's work
touches on various Christian traditions in Appalachian America including Pentecostalism. McCauley explains that most Christian mountainous people know the Bible primarily as oral literature. She adds that
they know the Bible very well, even if they cannot read. As a result of being primarily illiterate, Appalachian Christians have "highly developed
listening skills . . . compensating extremely well for whatever lapses in

---

18. W. Hollenweger, "The Pentecostal Elites and the Pentecostal Poor: A Missed
Dialogue?" in *Charismatic Christianity as a Global Culture*, ed. Karla Poewe (Columbia:
University of South Carolina 1994) 201.

19. Hollenweger, "Pentecostal Elites and the Pentecostal Poor," 213. The first generation would be included in his understanding of the "poor" which he contrasts with the
contemporary elite Pentecostals. The elites are those who are "literary conceptual peoples
who pride themselves on speaking the language of science and technology" (213).

20. Deborah McCauley, *Appalachian Mountain Religion: A History* (Chicago: University of Illinois Press, 1995).

21. Ibid., 195.

literacy."[22] McCauley finds that Appalachian Christian folk who desire to learn to read do so in order to read the Bible. Important is the reality that Pentecostalism's roots in the USA are entrenched in the slave Christianity of the South (the Mississippi Delta) and in the mountainous regions of the United States.[23]

Like early Pentecostals, current Pentecostals who come from the margins of society are predominantly oral/aural learners. They do theology primarily in narrative forms. Thus, to do theology in a manner that is consistent with our early tradition, a post-critical narrative method should be employed. Perhaps by allowing our theological explanations to be framed by narrative, we will better spiritually form our congregations into dynamic Pentecostal communities of the Spirit and the Word.[24]

Pentecostal theologian Frank Macchia rightly notes "Pentecostals have always favored testimonies, choruses and prayers over intellectual or critical reflection as the means by which to interpret the gospel."[25] Macchia suggests that Pentecostalism at its grass roots did theology in a narrative manner with a devotional tone, yet he finds Hollenweger's concept of orality too restrictive. Macchia correctly points out that early Pentecostals also wrote out testimonies and silently danced before the Lord. Because of these other forms, Macchia suggests that early Pentecostal theology should be classified as "nonacademic" instead of "oral." For Macchia "nonacademic" is not a bad or misguided or even an improper form of theology. "Nonacademic" serves as a descriptive category for early forms of Pentecostal theology that is more devotional and popularistic. Macchia uses "nonacademic" as a way of contrasting early grass roots Pentecostal theology with that which is conceptual, rationalistic, systematic, and

22. Ibid., 61–62, 76, 167, 382.

23. All early Pentecostal denominations have their headquarters in areas less affected by modernization such as mountainous regions like the Appalachian region (Church of God, Cleveland, TN), the Ozarks (Assembly of God, Springfield, MO) and the Mississippi Delta region (Church of God in Christ, Memphis, TN).

24. See Jackie David Johns and Cheryl Bridges Johns, "Yielding to the Spirit: A Pentecostal Approach to Group Bible Study," *Journal of Pentecostal Theology* 1 (1992) 109–34, for a critical approach to group "Bible Study" that takes the narrative form "testimony" as an essential element in this transformative communal learning activity.

25. Frank Macchia, "Theology, Pentecostal," in *New International Dictionary of Pentecostal and Charismatic Movements*, ed. Stanley M. Burgess (Grand Rapids: Zondervan, 2002) 1120–41, esp. 1120.

scholastic in form—the "modernistic" academically acceptable scientific manner.[26]

By "nonacademic," Macchia refers to theology that takes the forms of prayers, commentaries, devotional writings, and disputations. From this perspective, nonacademic theology is not necessarily concerned with critical reflection, contextualization or even methodological procedure. Macchia believes that these nonacademic forms are important and acceptable ways of doing theology that deserve to have a place alongside the scientific academic form. He writes, "The most creative Pentecostal theological discourse can be included as a more-or-less popular form of nonacademic theological genre."[27]

I agree with Macchia's assessment that early Pentecostal theology was more devotional and popularistic in tone. However, I find Macchia's descriptive concept of "nonacademic" problematic. I am concerned with the assessing of early Pentecostalism's ways of doing theology, both the forms and the content. We need critically to assess our grass roots and current works. Yet, by utilizing the concept of "nonacademic" as a means to classify early Pentecostal theology, Macchia undermines his argument that these forms have a place on the same shelf next to the academic forms. Nonacademic forms will be seen as lacking intellectual credence. The nonacademic will always be subordinate to the academic and be shelved beneath it (if found at all in the library). Further, those practitioners of the privileged academic (scholastic and or systematic) form will not take serious theology labeled "nonacademic."

I believe "pietistic" may serve as a more helpful descriptive category than "nonacademic."[28] Pietistic literature can be unsophisticated and popularistic; or it can be academically sophisticated in form, but remain a personal confessional extension of one's intimate, yet, communal relationship with the living God. For Pentecostals, this would reinforce the importance of a holistic embodied theology that integrates the head and

---

26. Macchia's notion of "nonacademic" comes from Karl Barth's description of German Pietism.

27. Macchia, "Theology, Pentecostal," 1121.

28. "Pietistic" also has problems and maybe it would be better to classify early Pentecostal literature as "paramodern." Early Pentecostalism was a paramodern movement because it existed on the fringes of modern society, see Kenneth J. Archer, *A Pentecostal Hermeneutic for the Twenty-First Century: Spirit, Scripture and Community* (New York: T. & T. Clark, 2004) 29–33.

hands into the heart.[29] Pentecostalism is an affective-experiential theological tradition, and to keep it as such we need an integrative methodology contextualized in an actual worshipping community.[30]

Our theological explanations can become a critical reflection upon our doxology with our acts of worship always informing and transforming our official dogma; and, in turn, our dogma informing our doxology. Orthodoxy has more to do with our primary way of doing theology, which is worship, than the secondary critical reflective activity—the production of official dogma or right believing (*orthopistis*). Worship is our primary way of doing theology.[31]

METHOD: INTEGRATIVE

A Pentecostal theological method should attempt to integrate orthopraxis and orthopistis into ortho-pathos. Praxis is an epistemological view which unites theory and practice. Actions give rise to and shape beliefs, and beliefs shape and inform activities. Praxis embraces the notion that theory and practice are really inseparable and mutually informing. This is contrary to much of the Western philosophical tradition which insists that theory must proceed first in order to provide the foundational rationale for practice. "Instead of theory leading to practice, theory becomes, or is seen in, the reflective moment in praxis." From this perspective "theory arises from praxis to wield further praxis."[32] Praxis, then, dialectically unites practice (doing) and theory (knowing) into the same activity. Even

---

29. The heart symbolizes the seat of our affections and affirms the important contribution of aesthetics to theological understanding. Steve Land argues for the integration of orthodoxy (right praise / belief) and orthopraxy (right action) into orthopathy (right affection). This is not a balancing act between feelings and thoughts but an integrative work wrought by the Holy Spirit; see *Pentecostal Spirituality: A Passion for the Kingdom*, 131–33. However, Land's proposal needs to become more explicitly communal and less individual.

30. The method and message should be understood as a manifestation of our tradition emanating from our contextualized Christian community. The Pentecostal theologian's first priority is an actual localized Christian community in which he or she actively engages in worship and ministry.

31. See Donald E. Saliers, *Worship As Theology: Foretaste of Glory Divine* (Nashville: Abingdon, 1994) especially chapter 2, "Dogma and Doxa," 39–48.

32. Cheryl Bridges Johns, *Pentecostal Formation: A Pedagogy among the Oppressed* (Sheffield, UK: Sheffield Academic Press, 1993) 37. See also Johns and Johns, "Yielding to the Spirit," 119–24.

though praxis is an important epistemological corrective, by itself, it is not enough to nurture a mature Pentecostal theology.

Hispanic Pentecostal theologian Samuel Solivan argues for a conjunctive integrative theology that places "orthopathos" as the interlocutor between orthopraxy and orthodoxy.[33] He understands orthopathos to be a necessary aspect of doing theology for two important reasons. First, North American theologians who embrace a praxis methodology are often detached from the very community for which they are doing theology—the poor and marginalized. They critically reflect upon someone else's suffering from an indirect detached position. Orthopathos moves the theologian into the community on the margins where suffering is a reality. This involvement among and with those who suffer gives the theologian a firsthand, direct existential engagement as one among and with the marginalized: "*Orthopathos* as an interlocutor seeks to or links us in community with those who suffer."[34] In this way orthopathos affirms the importance of a personal, yet, communal experiential theology and helps us to come into tune with the very pathos of God.[35]

Second, orthopathos provides a necessary corrective to the narrower, conservative, modernistic view of orthodoxy as correct propositional truth claims. This disembodied cognitive orthodoxy (theory) does not necessarily lead to the biblically affirmed responsibility of Christian social ministry to the poor (practice). As Solivan points out, history testifies that orthodox doctrine does not necessarily concern itself with the widow and the poor and often serves to legitimize the power structures favoring the status quo.[36] Orthopathos is the necessary corrective for either orthodoxy or orthopraxy because it brings an emphatic concern for those who are suffering into the very activity of doing theology.[37] When we lose

---

33. Samuel Solivan, *Spirit, Pathos and Liberation: Toward an Hispanic Pentecostal Theology* (Sheffield, UK: Sheffield Academic Press, 1998) 11, 68. Solivan raises important corrective concerns that help enhance both Johns' and Land's contributions by anchoring orthopathy in community and affirming the epistemological value of an experiential praxis of living in the margins.

34. Solivan, *Spirit, Pathos and Liberation*, 37.

35. Ibid., 38, writes, "God's self-disclosure in Jesus the Christ serves as a tangible paradigm of correspondence between God's *orthopathos* and the possibility of our own. The incarnation, death and resurrection of Christ and the giving of the Holy Spirit serve as principal examples of God's orthopathic character."

36. Ibid., 11, 35–36, 64–65.

37. Ibid., 60.

the experiential existential sense of what it means to be the marginalized that comes with actually living among the poor, we will give precedence to cognitive doctrine detached from the very pathos of God. We assume the epistemological argument that right theory (doctrine) produces right activity (ethics).

I agree with Solivan's argument that orthopathos puts us in touch with the compassionate redemptive liberation of Jesus Christ and the Holy Spirit. This redemptive liberation is anchored in the very passion of God manifested paradigmatically in the ministry of Jesus and the ongoing work of the Christian community empowered and impassioned by the Spirit. We must do theology from a conjunctive methodology that takes seriously orthopathos as the integrative center for our Pentecostal theology without setting aside either praxis or dogma. Without orthopathy, contemporary North American Pentecostalism will become the very community that early Pentecostals protested against—a cold, creedal and cerebral Christianity that has no room for the poor and hurting. Not to take pathos seriously would be to become disconnected from the very nature and mission of the Social Trinity.

MANNER: NARRATIVE

Not only must Pentecostal theology employ an integrative method, it must also articulate its theology in narrative forms. By using narrative we can produce critical theology for our present-day communities that are in continuity with the manner of the earliest Christians and early Pentecostals.

I understand "narrative" in two complementary ways. First, by narrative I mean to highlight the importance of understanding Scripture as a grand meta-narrative with the Gospels and Acts as the heart of the Christian story. Even though narrative is the predominant genre of Scripture, I am using narrative as a theological category. From this perspective, narrative is a way of grasping and making sense of the whole of God's inspired authoritative witness—Scripture.[38] The Social Trinity is the central figure of Christianity, with Jesus Christ being the very heart

---

38. For an informative explanation of the significance of narrative as a theological category for the understanding of Scripture see Joel B. Green, "The (Re-) Turn To Narrative," in *Narrative Reading, Narrative Preaching: Reuniting New Testament Interpretation and Proclamation*, eds. Joel B. Green and Michael Pasquarello (Grand Rapids: Baker Academic, 2003) 1–36.

of the story; therefore, a narrative theology will emphasize the priority of the Gospel of Jesus Christ and its significance for the Christian community and the world. This is not to suggest that a Pentecostal theology is unconcerned with other doctrinal themes, but it is to suggest that all doctrinal discussions in the end will come back to the theological center—the person Jesus Christ.[39]

Ted Peters, in his systematic theology entitled *God—the World's Future*, writes:

> If we were to think of Christian systematic theology as a wheel, the gospel of Jesus Christ would be located at the center. It is the hub around which everything else revolves . . . the gospel is that which establishes one's identity as Christian.[40]

Peters defines "gospel" as "the act of telling the story of Jesus with its significance." He further states that, "the gospel is the content of the story of Jesus and its significance; and this constitutes the material norm for systematic theology."[41] As a systematic theologian, Peters, like narrative theologians, recognizes the necessity of relating and integrating theological doctrines into the story of Jesus Christ.

Second, narrative provides a coherent and cohesive structure for articulating Pentecostal theology, which is simultaneously concerned about nurturing spirituality and Pentecostal identity. For Pentecostals, the significance of the story of Jesus is articulated through the proclamation of the "Full Gospel" or better, the "Fivefold Gospel."[42] Jesus is proclaimed as Savior, Sanctifier, Spirit Baptizer, Healer, and Coming King.[43]

---

39. Gerard Loughlin, *Telling God's Story: Bible, Church and Narrative Theology* (Cambridge: Cambridge University Press, 1996) preface. See also his essay, "The Basis and Authority of Doctrine," in *The Cambridge Companion to Doctrine*, ed. Colin E. Gunton (Cambridge: Cambridge University Press, 1997) 41–64, esp. 52–54.

40. Ted Peters, *God—The World's Future* (Minneapolis: Fortress, 1992) 43–44.

41. Ibid., 44.

42. See Donald Dayton, *Theological Roots of Pentecostalism* (Peabody, MA: Hendrickson, 1987). I am not suggesting that theological reflection is simply restating the Gospel. I believe all theological discourse is a secondary reflection on the primary source—the Scriptures—informed by experience, with the Gospel being the very heart of the Christian story.

43. See Donald Dayton, "Introduction," in *Transforming Power: Dimensions of the Gospel*, ed. Yung Chul Han (Cleveland: Pathway, 2001) 11–18. Dayton writes: "for a decade or so all of Pentecostalism was sharply Wesleyan/Holiness until this theme was suppressed by some under the influence of W. H. Durham" (13).

The Fivefold Gospel functions as the central narrative convictions of the Pentecostal community.[44] Pentecostals embrace the Full Gospel, which places Jesus and the Spirit at the center of God's dramatic redemptive story. Pentecostals, as the end-time people, are participating in the "Latter Rain" of this redemptive story. The proclamation of the Full Gospel is the declaration of the redemptive activity of God in Christ Jesus and the Holy Spirit to the community.

These confessional-doxological statements flow out of our redemptive encounter with the living Word, Jesus Christ, who is present in our community through the powerful presence of the Holy Spirit. We praise the Lord who saves, sanctifies, heals, Spirit baptizes, and is coming for us. The central narrative convictions of our story are doxological testimonies that shape our community.[45] Thus, the Fivefold Gospel is not a set of quaint platitudes but deep-seated, affectionate affirmations flowing from our worship of the living God who has transformed our lives. The Pentecostal story shapes our identity, guides our activity, and reflects our understanding of salvation for all of God's creation. For Pentecostals, then, our story with its central narrative convictions expressed through the Fivefold Gospel needs to take on a more overt role in our theological explanations. One important way of articulating a Pentecostal theology then would be to shape it around our story and structure it around the Fivefold Gospel.

Ted Peters' analogy of the "hub" works well for a Pentecostal theology structured around the Fivefold Gospel and centered upon Jesus Christ. The theological center is the person Jesus Christ, and protruding out of the center are the five spokes which serve to explain the significance of the story of Jesus Christ for the community and the world. These spokes are the central narrative convictions of the Pentecostal story. They are theological themes that bring coherence to the Pentecostal story and provide stability for the rest of Pentecostal theology. Our Pentecostal doctrinal practices and beliefs are the wheel, connected to and stabi-

---

44. I suggest that even for non-Wesleyan Pentecostals who are still holiness in orientation, sanctification would be a useful theological plank that could provide for a more dynamic synergistic soteriology that is inherent in Pentecostalism. For Pentecostals of all persuasions the pursuit of holiness in lifestyle is not an option but a command. The pneumatological dimension of sanctifying grace as an ontological participation in the Spirit helps further to develop a more robust Pentecostal theology.

45. For development of this argument, see chapter 2.

lized by the spokes, yet turning and spinning around its center—Jesus Christ. Pentecostal beliefs and practices, therefore, will always flow back to their center where they find their ultimate significance and justification—Jesus Christ.

Pentecostal theology should be written in a way that reflects the importance of Jesus Christ as articulated through the Fivefold Gospel.[46] John Christopher Thomas has creatively connected each doxological confession of Jesus with a particular biblical-sacramental sign. Thus, "Jesus is our Savior" is connected with the ecclesiastical rite of "water baptism," "Jesus is our Sanctifier" with "footwashing," Spirit Baptizer with *glossolalia* speech, Healer with praying for and anointing the sick with oil and Jesus as Coming King with the Lord's Supper. Thomas has set forth a proposal that is more integrative theologically by interconnecting ecclesiology and soteriology with Christology.[47]

One would need to articulate the Fivefold Gospel paradigm from an explicitly Spirit and Word understanding, however, so as not to eclipse or subordinate the necessary role and missional activity of the Spirit to Christ. The Pentecostal story could provide a coherent overall structure of the written work with each central narrative conviction becoming a point of intersection of and critical reflection on the various theological *loci*. In this way, ecclesiology, soteriology, and eschatology are held together around the missional story of the Social Trinity. For example, when discussing "Jesus Our Savior" one could discuss a pneumatic soteriology, eschatology, and then ecclesiology. To discuss "Jesus as Savior" and not embark upon a discussion that the Kingdom of God is breaking in among us and that through regeneration we become a part of a redeemed counter-cultural community is to misunderstand both the purpose of redemption and the very mission of Jesus Christ and the Spirit from a de-

---

46. I believe that the Pentecostal New Testament scholar John Christopher Thomas was the first to call for an integrative Pentecostal theology specifically structured around the Fivefold Gospel. See his "1998 Presidential Address: Pentecostal Theology in the Twenty-First Century," *PNEUMA* 20 (1998) 3–19, esp. 17–19. See also Veli-Matti Karkkainen, "David's Sling: The Promise and Problem of Pentecostal Theology Today: A Response to D. Lyle Dabney," *Pneuma* 23 (2001) 147–52. His comment, "I am drawn to the Pentecostal—Spirit-led, I am sure—focus on Jesus Christ as the center of the (five or fourfold) Gospel . . . it is a precious methodological gateway to a balanced theology" (152), resonates well with what I am proposing.

47. For a narrative expansion on Thomas' proposal and further development concerning the sacramental nature of the signs, see chapter 4.

cisively Pentecostal perspective. Just because the structure follows a more narrative format constructed around the Fivefold Gospel does not make it less academic or less intelligent or less capable of addressing concerns raised by the traditional theological *loci*.[48] Furthermore, a Pentecostal theology can avoid a Christomonistic tendency of Reformation theology of the Word by affirming and addressing the missional role of the Spirit in conjunction with the missional role of Jesus.[49] Spirit-Christology would more correctly reflect the Pentecostal story and scriptural testimony. It may not be classified as a "systematic theology," but it can be a fully orbed Pentecostal theology that adequately addresses the various theological themes arising out of the scriptural witness and fleshes out the dynamic interactions of the Spirit and Word.

In conclusion, Pentecostal theology must be done in a holistic integrative manner. We can be more creative in our articulation of the Gospel. This may lead to important insights missed by other traditions as well as necessitate a revision of our story.[50] Furthermore, a Pentecostal narrative theology would have immediate benefits for the Pentecostal community by shaping and reshaping its identity through a critical engagement of its story. A Pentecostal theology structured around the Fivefold Gospel would make an important contribution to the Pentecostal communities, but not necessarily the definitive contribution. For, surely, the Spirit has more to say and ways to say it!

48. *Contra* Frank Macchia, who believes that the Full Gospel as a framework is unable to address the full spectrum of theological *loci*. Macchia writes "Such a framework is potentially Christomonistic (in which devotion to Christ defines every area of theological concern) and dominated by a concern with the way of salvation." Thus, for Macchia, "Pentecostal theology cannot be confined to this paradigm if it is to speak to a broader configuration of *loci*" ("Theology, Pentecostal," 1124). Interestingly, Macchia does lift up Karl Barth as an example for Pentecostals who want to move beyond "nonacademic" and scientific interpretive methodology. Macchia does not specifically say this, but I believe he is suggesting—the way Barth did—a theological interpretation (his method). Interestingly, Barth's work has been criticized for being "Christomonistic," which is the very thing Macchia wants to avoid, hence his rejection of the Fivefold Gospel as an organizational narrative for a Pentecostal theology (1123).

49. The growing interest in Spirit-Christology signals the necessity to rethink both pneumatology and Christology. See Ralph Del Colle's important Roman Catholic contribution to a renewed Spirit-Christology: *Christ and the Spirit: Spirit-Christology in Trinitarian Perspective* (New York: Oxford University Press, 1994).

50. See Richard Shaull, "From Academic Research to Spiritual Transformation: Reflections on a study of Pentecostalism in Brazil," *PNEUMA* 20 (1998) 71–84.

Pentecostal Story

The Hermeneutical Filter for the Making of Meaning[1]

Devoted saints come from the HOLINESS church, bringing the message of Heart-Purity and the Coming of the Lord, and wonderfully blessed of God, as fruitage needing but one thing—the latter rain.

—Aimee Semple McPherson[2]

HERMENEUTICS IS AN IMPORTANT subject for Pentecostals.[3] Generally, the hermeneutical concern has focused attention upon the proper use of an exegetical method with the assumption that methods are somehow the neutral and objective means of establishing the validity of one's doctrinal interpretation of Scripture.[4] For Pentecostals of all generations, the issue of biblical hermeneutics always arises whenever the doctrine of Spirit baptism is discussed.[5] Thus, the proper biblical interpretation

---

1. This is a revision of my paper entitled "Pentecostal Story as the Hermeneutical Filter," presented at the 30th Annual Meeting of the Society for Pentecostal Studies, March 8–10, 2001.

2. Aimee Semple McPherson, *This Is That* (Los Angeles: Echo Park Evangelistic, 1923) 787.

3. For some of the more recent articles on Pentecostal hermeneutics, see *The Spirit and the Church* 2 (2000), and Veli-Matti Kärkkäinen, "Pentecostal Hermeneutics in the Making: On the Way From Fundamentalism to Postmodernism," *Journal of the European Pentecostal Association* 18 (1998) 76–115.

4. See Kenneth J. Archer, "Pentecostal Hermeneutics: Retrospect and Prospect," *Journal of Pentecostal Theology* 8 (1996) 63–81.

5. For example, Baptist theologian Stanley Grenz, in his *Theology for the Community of God* (Grand Rapids: Eerdmans, 2000), specifically challenges the Pentecostal view of

of Luke-Acts has become the primary front in the battle, with both sides believing that the war can be won by exegetically demonstrating either the inadequacy or the adequacy of the Pentecostal doctrine.[6] When the discussion shifts from the so-called distinctive doctrine of Spirit baptism to whether or not there even exists an authentic "Pentecostal" theology, hermeneutical concerns surface again in the disguise of theological method. It is no wonder hermeneutics continues to be an important topic at the annual meetings of the Society for Pentecostal Studies.

The contemporary hermeneutical concern recognizes that the use of exegetical-theological methods must take into consideration the social-cultural location of the person using it.[7] The hermeneuts and the methods are not isolated islands. Both the methods and the hermeneuts are socially, culturally, and theologically shaped entities that contribute to the making of meaning.[8] In order for interpretation to take place, the reader must participate. Readers are not neutral observers; instead, they are engaged by the text. "Reading involves using both the information that is present on the written page, as well as, the information we already have

---

Spirit baptism (the only community he directly takes on in this theological work) on grounds that Pentecostals have misunderstood the genre of Acts, misread the Luke-Acts accounts, and cannot anchor their doctrine in the Pauline epistles. His charge is a restatement of the typical evangelical position. He offers three reasons for his rejection of the Pentecostal understanding of Spirit baptism as experience subsequent to regeneration. They are: (1) Pentecost as recorded in Acts 2 was a one-time non-repeatable event; thus, one is Spirit-baptized at the moment of regeneration (419, 422); (2) Acts is primarily a historical document: "Historical narrative alone is not necessarily a sure foundation for doctrine" unless it can be "confirmed by the Epistles" (421); Finally, Grenz appeals to the Apostle Paul's writings, and because he cannot find the doctrine in "the explicit teaching of Paul" he rejects it (421). For a penetrating look into the origin of "initial evidence" see Gary McGee, ed., *Initial Evidence: Historical and Biblical Perspectives on Pentecostal Doctrine of Spirit Baptism* (Peabody, MA: Hendrickson, 1991) chap. 6.

6. Simon Chan, in *Pentecostal Theology and the Christian Tradition* (Sheffield, England: Sheffield Academic Press, 2000), correctly moves the discussion about "initial evidence" from the exegetical readings of Acts and Paul into a more robust theological integration into the Christian life. While he believes that exegesis cannot demonstrate the validity of tongues speech as *the* sign of Spirit baptism, he does argue that tongues can be shown to be the most natural and spontaneous response of Spirit- baptism experience, and he does so by approaching the issue from a broader theological perspective. See esp. chap. 2, "Glossolalia as Initial Evidence," 40–72.

7. Bernard C. Lategan, "Hermeneutics," in *The Anchor Bible Dictionary*, vol. 3 (New York: Doubleday, 1992) 153–54.

8. See Justo L. Gonzalez, *Santa Biblia: The Bible Through Hispanic Eyes* (Nashville: Abingdon, 1996).

in our minds." The reader does not come to the text as a blank slate.[9] Comprehension of a written text involves both a discovery and a creation of meaningful understanding.[10] Therefore, the way in which Pentecostals or any community goes about doing "exegesis" and "theology" has as much to do with their social location and theological formation as it does with their employment of a so-called neutral, scientific, exegetical-theological methodology. The role of the hermeneut in the interpretive process must also be considered. This touches upon the issue of community and identity.

What distinguished the early Pentecostal community from the Holiness folk was not their exegetical method,[11] nor simply the so-called unique doctrine of Spirit baptism;[12] rather, what distinguished the Pentecostal community from other Christian communities was their distinct narrative—a particular twist on the Christian story. The Pentecostal movement's continuation of Holiness praxis in confrontation with cessationist fundamentalism and experiential liberalism created a fertile context in which an authentic Pentecostal story could emerge. The Pentecostal story is the glue that holds the similar, acceptable exegetical-theological methods together in a coherent and cohesive interpretive manner. The Pentecostal hermeneutic at the foundational interpretive level is its unique story. In the remainder of this chapter, I will identify the theological story of the Pentecostal community and show how that story has shaped the hermeneut-in-community and how this in turn enables the making of theological meaning.

9. Jeff McQuillian, *The Literary Crisis: False Claims, Real Solutions* (Portsmouth, NH: Heinemann, 1998) 16.

10. See George Aichele et al., *The Postmodern Bible: The Bible and Culture Collective* (New Haven, CT: Yale University Press, 1995) 1–8, which challenges the notion of the Enlightenment's control of objectivity and stability of meaning..

11. See Kenneth J. Archer, "Early Pentecostal Biblical Interpretation," *Journal of Pentecostal Theology* 18 (2001) 79–117. I explain the early Pentecostal exegetical method as the "Bible Reading Method." The Bible Reading Method was a paramodern common-sense approach to interpretation that utilized inductive and deductive reasoning skills.

12. Spirit baptism is, of course, vitally necessary for an authentic Pentecostal spirituality. I agree with De Kock's observation that Spirit baptism is not "the sum total of Pentecostal spirituality [theology]." Wynand J. De Kock, "Pentecostal Power for a Pentecostal Task: Empowerment through Engagement in South African Context," *Journal of Pentecostal Theology* 16 (2000) 108.

COMMUNITY STORY AND INTERPRETATION

Harry Stout has demonstrated that there is an inescapable relationship between the community to which one belongs and the way in which one explains past religious history.[13] In his essay, "Theological Commitment and American Religious History," Stout addresses the issue of the historian's commitment to a community and its influence upon the telling of American Christian history.

In examining two prominent non-Christian historians of Puritanism, Perry Miller and Edmund S. Morgan, Stout demonstrates that one's theological or non-theological commitment affects neither one's choice to pursue a religious subject, nor one's ability to be empathetic concerning the subjects being studied. Further, there is no difference in the selection and use of critical methods or critical sources. Stout is convinced that "on the level of method and sympathy for the subject there is no connection between atheistic commitment and religious history writing."[14] Stout does believe, however, that one's commitment to a particular community does shape the telling of religious history in decisive ways because the view of the observer is connected to the "common memory" of the particular community to which he or she is "internally bound."[15] He argues that it is the deeper level of philosophical commitment, or the historian's "point of view," that "directs the script and selects the themes in ways that invariably point back to the ultimate values of the story-tellers" (i.e., the historians).[16]

Drawing upon the work of H. Richard Niebuhr, Stout argues that the storyteller's point of view allows for "an existential relationship between the individual and his/her subject that stays with writers throughout their work. Insofar as all history writing involves an ongoing dialectic between the subject/actors and historian observer, the view of the observer does make a difference."[17] The historian who observes is caught up in an existential dialectic between subject/actor and being a historian/observer; hence "history stories are neither past nor present, but both simultane-

13. Harry S. Stout, "Theological Commitment and American Religious History," *Theological Education* 25 (1989) 44–59.

14. Ibid., 47.

15. Ibid., 48.

16. Ibid., 52.

17. Ibid., 47–48.

ously," and this results in a "participatory history."[18] One's point of view inevitably shapes the story and guides both the methodological analysis being used and the interpretation of the analysis.

A person's "point of view," as Stout calls it, is formed by that individual's participation in a community. The historian's or biblical scholar's point of view guides the methodological critical analysis and inevitably shapes the present retelling of past history. The "point of view," as discussed by Stout, could also be understood as the narrative tradition of the community with which the historian is presently affiliated. Therefore, the narrative tradition of a community becomes an essential part of any hermeneutical strategy, for the making and explaining of meaning is inherently communal.

PENTECOSTAL STORY AS A HERMENEUTICAL NARRATIVE TRADITION

Alasdair MacIntyre, a philosophical ethicist, has had a major impact upon the understanding of moral reasoning.[19] MacIntyre, unlike the "Enlightenment Project," argues that all moral reasoning takes place from within a particular narrative tradition. He demonstrates that interpretive practices of a community are always dependent upon the community's narrative tradition. The narrative tradition provides the context in which moral reason, along with its interpretive practices, can be understood.[20]

MacIntyre's concept of narrative as a descriptive category is difficult to grasp because of the different and, at times, contradictory ways he employs it.[21] But it nonetheless plays a central role in his understanding of moral reasoning. In fact, his argument concerning moral reasoning relies upon the interaction of four major concepts: narrative, tradition, virtue, and practice.[22] For my purpose here, however, I will only be concerned

---

18. Ibid., 48.

19. See, e.g., Nancey Murphy, Brad Kallenberg, and Mark Nation, eds., *Virtues and Practices in the Christian Tradition: Christian Ethics after MacIntyre* (Harrisburg, PA: Trinity, 1997).

20. See Alasdair MacIntyre, *After Virtue: A Study in Moral Theory*, 2nd ed. (Notre Dame: University of Notre Dame Press, 1984). Also see MacIntyre's sequel, *Whose Justice? Which Rationality* (Notre Dame: University of Notre Dame Press, 1988).

21. L. Gregory Jones, "Alasdair MacIntyre on Narrative, Community, and the Moral Life," *Modern Theology* 4 (1987) 53.

22. Brad J. Kallenberg, "The Master Argument of MacIntyre's *After Virtue*," in *Virtues and Practices in the Christian Tradition*, 20.

about narrative. One of MacIntyre's central theses is that "man is in his actions and practices, as well as in his fictions, essentially a story-telling animal." Therefore, "I can only answer the question 'What am I to do?' if I can answer the prior question, 'of what story or stories do I find myself a part?'"[23] MacIntyre's primary concern has been to demonstrate that "dramatic narrative is the crucial form for an understanding of human action" and moral reasoning.[24]

According to L. Gregory Jones, there are two principles that underlie MacIntyre's diverse descriptions of narrative: historicity and human action.[25] Jones states, "What MacIntyre is concerned to establish in all the uses of narrative is their historical character. . . . MacIntyre believes that human action, in order to be intelligible, requires an account of a context which only a true dramatic narrative can provide."[26] Therefore, any interpretive method with its epistemological system is "inescapably historically and socially context bound" and is "inseparable from the intellectual and social tradition in which it is embodied."[27] Furthermore, the community's narrative envelops the tradition and makes the methodological argument understandable and meaningfully acceptable.[28] The "community," then, "is the bearer, interpreter and concert expression of its tradition."[29]

Does this lead, then, to relative pluralism? No, it just emphasizes that all moral reasoning is dependent upon and takes place within a narrative tradition. Nancey Murphy writes: "MacIntyre has complex and ingenious arguments to show that, despite the tradition-dependence of all specific moral arguments, it is nonetheless possible to make respectable public claims, showing one tradition of moral reasoning to be superior to its rivals."[30] Trevor Hart further explains how MacIntyre's account of moral reasoning challenges relativism. MacIntyre is "reminding us that

23. MacIntyre, *After Virtue*, 216.

24. Alasdair MacIntyre, "Epistemological Crises, Dramatic Narrative, and the Philosophy of Science," in *Why Narrative? Readings in Narrative Theology*, eds. Stanley Hauerwas and L. Gregory Jones (Grand Rapids: Eerdmans, 1989) 150.

25. Jones, "Alasdair MacIntyre on Narrative, Community, and the Moral Life," 57.

26. Ibid.

27. MacIntyre, *Whose Justice? Which Rationality*, 4, 8.

28. Jones, "Alasdair MacIntyre on Narrative, Community, and the Moral Life." Jones challenges MacIntyre for his lack of emphasis upon community, 59.

29. Kallenberg, "Master Argument of MacIntyre's *After Virtue*," 64.

30. *Virtues and Practices in the Christian Tradition*, 2.

traditions are rooted in communities, and thereby reinforcing the suggestion that rationality, far from being an isolated and uniquely personal or subjective thing, is in fact an interpersonal matter as well." Narrative traditions, then, "are justified by their supposed appropriateness as accounts of reality. They refer us appropriately to the world, and facilitate a meaningful engagement with it in its rich diversity." MacIntyre, then, "is not a relativist but a realist."[31]

At this point, I need to clarify how I understand the Pentecostal narrative tradition and its relationship to Christianity. The Pentecostal community is a distinct coherent narrative tradition within Christianity. Pentecostal communities are bound together by their charismatic experiences and common story. The Pentecostal narrative tradition is one embodiment of the Christian metanarrative.[32] Yet, because the Pentecostal community understands itself to be a restorational movement, it has argued that it is the best representation or embodiment of Christianity in the world today. This may sound triumphalist; yet, Pentecostals, like all restorational narrative traditions of Christianity, desire to be both an authentic continuation of New Testament Christianity and a faithful representation of New Testament Christianity in the present societies in which they exist.[33] Of course, the understanding of what was and should be New Testament Christianity is based upon a Pentecostal understanding. Moral reasoning, which includes biblical-theological interpretation, is contextualized in the narrative tradition of the Pentecostal community.

31. Trevor Hart, *Faith Thinking: The Dynamics of Christian Theology* (London: Society for Promoting Christian Knowledge, 1995) 68. See also MacIntyre, *Whose Justice? Which Rationality*. "Post-Enlightenment relativism and perspectivism are thus the negative counterpart of Enlightenment, its inverted mirror image," 353.

32. By metanarrative I am referring to a grand story by which human societies and their individual members live and organize their lives in meaningful ways. The Christian metanarrative refers to the general Christian story about the meaning of the world, the God who created it, and humanity's place in it. This is a story that begins with a good creation, includes a fall into sin, redemption through the Messiah, Christian community, and final restoration of all creation. The Christian metanarrative is primarily dependent on the Bible for this general narrative. For a basic outline of the "Storyline" of the Christian metanarrative, see Gabriel Fackre, *The Christian Story: A Narrative of Basic Christian Doctrine*, vol. 1, 3rd ed. (Grand Rapids: Eerdmans, 1996). Fackre writes that "Creation, Fall, Covenant, Jesus Christ, Church, Salvation, Consummation, . . . are acts in the Christian drama," with the understanding that "there is a God who creates, reconciles, and redeems the word" as "the "Storyline" (8–9).

33. Pentecostals see themselves as continuing the reformation process of Protestantism.

Pentecostals will engage Scripture, do theology, and reflect upon reality from their own contextualized communities and narrative tradition.[34]

PENTECOSTAL STORY AND THE MAKING OF MEANING

The Pentecostal story or narrative tradition is the primary hermeneutical context for the production of theological meaning. The Pentecostal narrative tradition provides Pentecostals with an experiential, conceptual hermeneutical narrative that enables them to interpret Scripture and their experience of reality. The Pentecostal narrative tradition is the hermeneutical horizon of the community and the means of articulating its identity.

The community story is essential for shaping and communicating identity. Trevor Hart explains, "Stories . . . are very important to our identity as human beings in community. Every human community has a story which it tells both itself and others concerning its distinct origins and raison d'être, and about the sort of place this world in which it exists is."[35] The Pentecostal narrative tradition is an eschatological Christian story of God's involvement in the restoration of the Christian community and God's dramatic involvement both in reality and the Pentecostal community.[36]

The Pentecostal community's identity is forged from its reading of the biblical narrative of Acts and then the Gospels. Pentecostals desire to live as the eschatological people of God. They are caught up in the final drama of God's redemptive activity, which is channeled through Jesus and manifested in the community by the Holy Spirit, and they enthusiastically embrace and proclaim the Full Gospel.[37] This places Jesus at the heart of

---

34 MacIntyre, *Whose Justice? Which Rationality,* 354. Concerning contextualization, see Gonzalez, *Santa Biblia:* "Contextualization may certainly lead to fragmentation but is not necessarily its result. *Unconscious* contextualization, on the other hand, will certainly lead to fragmentation. . . . What leads to fragmentation is lack of recognition that all these theologies, as well as all expressions of traditional theology, are contextual, and therefore express the gospel as seen from a particular perspective" (17).

35. Hart, *Faith Thinking,* 107.

36. This will be presented later in this essay.

37. The Full Gospel is the Pentecostals' doxological confession concerning Jesus as Savior, Sanctifier, Healer, Spirit Baptizer, and Soon Coming King. This confession is the very heart of Pentecostal ethos. Donald Dayton has demonstrated that the Full Gospel forms the basic *gestalt* of Pentecostal thought and rhetoric. See Donald Dayton, *Theological Roots of Pentecostalism* (Peabody, MA: Hendrickson, 1987) 173.

God's dramatic story, which in turn emphasizes the missionary role of the community.

The Pentecostal community reads Scripture from a Pentecostal perspective shaped by its particular story. As in all readings, there will be a transaction between the biblical text and the community, and this will result in the production of meaning. Therefore, there exists a dialectic encounter between two poles: the biblical text and the community. This encounter is possible because within the biblical story and the Pentecostal community there are a number of working plots.

Dan Hawk explains how plot functions on a number of levels. A plot exists on the surface level of the story, and in this sense, plot "may refer to the framework of the story."[38] Plot can also refer to the more detailed "arrangement of incidents and patterns as they relate to each other" in a story. These two functions of plot recognize that it operates within the self-contained world of a biblical narrative. Nevertheless, Hawk also argues that there exist real yet abstract notions of plot operating within the mind of the reader. The reader then also "exercises a tendency to organize and make connections between events." According to Hawk, this function of plot in the mind of the reader is a "dynamic phenomenon" that "moves beyond the formal aspects of the text and addresses the interpretive processes that take place between text and reader."[39] This happens because a "narrative . . . elicits a dynamic interpretative relationship between text and reader."[40] This understanding of plot affirms an existential intertextual phenomenon that makes the act of communication possible between text and reader.

When the Pentecostal in community reads Scripture, he or she will place the biblical stories into the cohesive Pentecostal narrative tradition. This is not simply a linear process. Pentecostals will allow for the biblical stories to challenge and reshape their understanding and even their tradition, because Scripture is understood to be the authoritative source and norm for theologizing.

The dialogical and dialectical encounter between the Bible and the community makes the making of meaning possible. This implies that the making of meaning and the validation of that meaning will take place

---

38. L. Daniel Hawk, *Every Promised Fulfilled: Contesting Plots in Joshua* (Louisville: Westminster John Knox, 1991) 19. Hawk is drawing upon Paul Ricoeur.

39. Hawk, *Every Promised Fulfilled*, 27.

40. Ibid.

primarily within the community; thus, authoritative meaning rests in the pragmatic decision of the community.[41] The community must discern what the text means and how that meaning is to be lived out in the community. This decision-making process is imperative for Pentecostals, because Pentecostal interpretation includes an act of willful obedient response to the Scripture's meaning.

THEOLOGICAL PRECURSORS FOR THE EMERGENCE OF THE PENTECOSTAL STORY

The purpose of this section is to identify two essential theological influences that enabled the Pentecostal community and its unique story to come into existence. This will be accomplished first by demonstrating the impact that the latter rain motif had upon early Pentecostal identity and how that theological concept set the stage for the "restoration" of the Full Gospel, which gave birth to the Pentecostal community.

THE LATTER RAIN MOTIF

D. William Faupel has demonstrated that the latter rain motif provides the primary organizational structure for the Pentecostal narrative tradition.[42] Thus, the early Pentecostal exegetical method, although similar to the other budding popularistic evangelical traditions, differs because the Pentecostals held to a distinct narrative in which the latter rain motif played a significant role in the fabrication of the Pentecostal story.[43] The latter rain motif also provided the early Pentecostals with an important organizational and relational role in the interpretive process; in other words, it enabled Pentecostals to relate and interpret the Old and New Testament intertextually according to a promise-fulfillment strategy. The

---

41. See Stanley Fish, *Is There a Text in This Class? The Authority of Interpretive Communities* (Cambridge: Harvard University Press, 1980). Fish left formalistic thinking about texts and here argues that communities write texts in the very act of reading. I do not totally agree with Fish's pragmatic view that communities dominate and use texts as they see fit, but Fish is correct in his argument that interpretive communities do have the final decision in proclaiming what a text means.

42. *The Everlasting Gospel: The Significance of Eschatology in the Development of Pentecostal Thought* (Sheffield: Sheffield Academic, 1996) see chap. 2, 19–43.

43. The biblical references used to develop the early and latter rain motifs were Deut 11:10–15; Job 29:29; Prov 16:15; Jer 3:3, 5:24; Hosea 6:3; Joel 2:23; Zech 10:1, and James 5:7.

promise-fulfillment strategy also allowed them to extend the biblical promise(s) into their present community thus enabling them to participate in the past promises, presently. G. F. Taylor explained the significance of the latter rain motif as follows:

> God fashioned the land of Palestine to be the model land of all lands, to contain the products of all zones and climates, to be a miniature world in itself, and so He arranged the coming and going of its rain clouds on a spiritual pattern, to beautifully adumbrate the movements of the Holy Spirit. So just what the rain is to the earth, the Holy Spirit is to the soul. God arranged the showers of rain in the land of Canaan, as a type of the operations of grace. Many Scriptures allude to the early and latter rain, and these are used as types of the Holy Spirit.[44]

The early and latter rain motif is based upon the typical weather cycle in Palestine and the biblical promise that God would provide the necessary rain for a plentiful harvest (the former and latter rains) if Israel remained faithful to its covenant relationship with Yahweh.[45] The latter rain motif provided the Pentecostal community with a stable conceptual framework through which it interpreted God's involvement with the whole of human history. It "provided the broad framework in which the Pentecostal world-view could be constructed."[46] Therefore, the latter rain motif played a prominent role in the fashioning of the narrative tradition of the early Pentecostal community by providing the basic structure for the Pentecostal story.

Latter rain terminology was common among the various Holiness groups.[47] People were praying for and expecting a great outpouring of

---

44. Taylor, *The Spirit and the Bride* (ca. 1907), 90. He dedicated chapter 9 of this work to the explanation of the early and Latter Rain (90–99).

45. See A. H. Joy, "Rain," in *The International Standard Bible Encyclopedia*, ed. J. Orr (Chicago: Howard Severance, 1915) 4:25–26. Faupel (*Everlasting Gospel*, 30) points out that the Pentecostals misunderstood the Palestinian weather cycle. They thought that the early and latter rain pattern took place before and then after the hot dry North American summer, thus a spring and then a fall rain. Actually it takes place during the winter rainy season of Palestine, with October being the early rain and April being the latter rain.

46. Faupel, *Everlasting Gospel*, 35–36. See 32–36 for an important discussion on the significance of the latter rain motif's contribution to the structure of the Pentecostal message. See also Edith Blumhofer, *Restoring the Faith: The Assemblies of God, Pentecostalism, and American Culture* (Chicago: University of Illinois Press, 1999) 93–97, for a discussion of the influence of the latter rain concept upon the lifestyle of the early Pentecostals.

47. Blumhofer (*Restoring the Faith*, 96) argues that "proto-fundamentalists" such as A. T. Pierson prayed for the latter rain outpouring and "diligently" charted the rainfall pat-

God's Spirit at the turn of the twentieth century. They longed for the promised latter rain, which would bring in the end-time harvest and, thus, assure the coming of the Lord. A. B. Simpson, founder of the Christian and Missionary Alliance (CMA), wrote in his denominational magazine:

> We may . . . conclude that we are to expect a great outpouring of the Holy Spirit in connection with the second coming of Christ and one as much greater than the Pentecostal effusion [Acts 2] as the rains of autumn were greater than the showers of spring. . . . We are in the time . . . when we may expect this latter rain.[48]

Simpson, like many at the turn of the century, was praying and longing for the eschatological fulfillment of Joel's prophecy, which, he and others believed, was beginning to take place. They had already begun to experience a sprinkling of the latter rain showers (sanctification, divine healing, and premillennialism). Because the "early rain" (Acts 2) empowered the early Church with supernatural gifts, Simpson and those who did not embrace a cessationist view expected a full and greater restoration of all the gifts during the latter rain just prior to the second coming of Christ.[49]

---

terns of Palestine; yet, unlike the Pentecostals, "[proto-fundamentalists] did not expect the full recurrence of apostolic "signs." I disagree with Blumhofer's statement, because there existed within her "proto-fundamentalist" coalition those traditions and people who were cessationist, like Keswickian dispensationalist A. T. Pierson, and those like A. B. Simpson, who were Keswickian but not cessationist. Thus, whether or not you expect miracles to be restored to the Church depends upon whether or not you are a cessationist. Also, the Wesleyan Holiness, Pentecostal, and proto-fundamentalists (cessationist and noncessationist) will predominantly embrace Scofield's dispensational hermeneutic (all Baptist fundamentalists had already done so), yet such noncessationists as the Pentecostals will modify in light of the latter rain narrative. Therefore, not all proto-fundamentalists were cessationist, and some, like A. B. Simpson, were praying for the restoration of all the supernatural gifts to the Church. Thus the term *proto-fundamentalist* adds more confusion than clarification concerning these early revivalist groups. A better way to classify such groups would be to recognize them as either cessationists or noncessationists in theological orientation.

48. Cited in Blumhofer, *Assemblies of God*, 151. For a very important presentation of A. B. Simpson's relationship with Pentecostalism, see Charles W. Nienkrichen, *A. B. Simpson and the Pentecostal Movement: A Study In Continuity, Crisis, and Change* (Peabody, MA: Hendrickson, 1992). Nienkrichen argues that the contemporary attitude of the current Christian Missionary Alliance denomination was primarily shaped by the latter revisionist interpretation of Simpson's writings by A. W. Tozer then by Simpson, himself.

49. For Simpson's understanding of the "latter rain" motif see Nienkrichen, *A. B. Simpson and the Pentecostal Movement*, 65–68. Nienkrichen correctly points out that

Pentecostals, however, seized the early and latter rain motif and utilized it as an apologetic explanation for the importance of their movement. The early rain was the outpouring of the Holy Spirit upon the first-century Christians at Pentecost as recorded in Acts 2. The latter rain was the outpouring of the Holy Spirit upon saved and sanctified Christians at the turn of the century. The time in between the early and latter rain was a time of drought caused by the "great apostasy" of the Roman Catholic Church.

The biblical latter rain motif became an important contribution to the Pentecostal story. In fact, there would be no Pentecostal story without it. The latter rain motif enabled the Pentecostals to hold together the Full Gospel message because it provided a coherent explanation for the restoration of the supernatural gifts, while also providing the primary organizational structure for their story. The Pentecostals became the people of the prophetically promised latter rain, which meant that they had fully recovered not only the apostolic faith, but also apostolic power, authority, *pathos,* and practice.[50]

Pentecostals often appealed to the manifestation of miracles as validation of their message. "Signs and wonders" became an important "proof" for validating the Pentecostal story, and with this came the development of a "signs theology." For example, in *The Apostolic Faith* under the banner "Signs Follow," one reads:

> The signs are following in Los Angeles. The eyes of the blind have been opened, the lame have been made to walk, and those who have accidentally drunk poison have been healed. One came suffering from poison and was healed instantly. Devils are cast out, and many speak in new tongues. All the signs in Mark 16:16–18 have followed except the raising of the dead, and we believe God will have someone to receive that power. We want all the signs that it may prove that God is true. It will result in the salvation of many souls.[51]

---

there is a logical corollary of Simpson's doctrine of "latter rain" and his emphasis upon the restoration of New Testament miracles, which "was his categorical rejection of cessationism," 66. Simpson would not embrace the normative argument of the Pentecostals concerning Spirit baptism as being evidenced by speaking in tongues, even though he was sympathetic to the movement and supportive of the manifestation of supernatural gifts, 129.

50. Faupel, *Everlasting Gospel,* 39.

51. Los Angeles, October 1906, vol. 1, number 3, p. 4.

The purpose of the latter rain outpouring was to bring the true Church to perfection and unity, while empowering the individual Christian with supernatural power in order to be a witness in these last days.[52] Thus, Myland said, "No matter how often you said, 'saved, sanctified, and healed,' you still need Pentecost."[53] The latter rain outpouring was "the fullness of the Spirit and the power of the Gospel of Christ restored."[54]

The primary candidates for the latter rain outpouring were the financially poor and outcast of society. Myland wrote:

> "Thou, O God, hast prepared of Thy goodness for the poor." . . . I don't know what the poor can do, the church has little use for them; but God sent this Latter Rain to gather up all the poor and outcast, and make us love everybody: feeble ones, base ones, those that have just been cast out of human society; no one wants them, all the outcasts of India and China; these are what God sent the Latter Rain people to pick up.[55]

The Pentecostals were marginalized people who heeded the call to empty themselves of "self-love" and "self-will" and immerse themselves in the latter rain outpouring, which was the restoration of the Gospel of Christ for the preparation and participation of the end-time harvest.[56]

In sum, the latter rain motif provided Pentecostals with a persuasive theological apologetic account for the existence of their community. The latter rain motif provided the basic structure for the Pentecostal story. The Pentecostal story brought together the Full Gospel message and extended the past biblical latter rain covenant of promise into the present Pentecostal movement. The Pentecostals, then, understood themselves as the prophetically promised eschatological community who would

52. D. Wesley Myland, *The Latter Rain Covenant and Pentecostal Power* (Chicago: Evangel, 1910) 29, 52, 88, 96, and 99.

53. Ibid., 61.

54. Ibid., 54.

55. Ibid., 53. See 84 where he argued that all who wanted to be used by God must become servants and handmaidens. See 113–14 where he condemns the wealthy non-Christian and 87 where he rebukes the Christian who has money. Myland proclaimed "If the Lord should burst through the air with the sound of the trump and voice of the archangel, many who profess to believe these truths could not go up to meet him because they are bound down by bank stocks, bonds, and real estate- these are weights upon them."

56. Ibid., 52. The Azusa Street revival was often compared to the humble surroundings of Christ's birth.

bring about the unity of Christianity and usher in the Second Coming of Christ.

PRIMITIVISTIC POSTURE

In this section I will explain the influences that motivated Pentecostals to read Scripture in a restorative manner. This is directly related to the importance and priority placed upon the Book of Acts and its harmonization with the rest of Scripture. Their community concerns were important in causing the Pentecostals to ask specific questions and look to Scripture for the answers.

Mark Noll has stated that the typical attitude of nineteenth-century conservatives toward Scripture was that "the Bible was a book to be studied *with* the history of the church, not *against* it."[57] Pentecostals knew that past church history lacked a consistent attestation of the supernatural gifts operating throughout Christianity. Rather than dissuading them, it reinforced the veracity of their claim. Pentecostals were convinced that they were simply returning to primitive Christianity and that they had restored the Full Gospel, which was "the restoration of the faith once delivered unto the saints."[58]

Pentecostal culture wholeheartedly embraced the pronouncements made by the influential Wesleyan Holiness leader John P. Brooks, who was the chief architect of "Come-outism." Brooks denounced all denominational churches as sects and declared that the true Church was to be found among the local Holiness churches.[59] Brooks was convinced that the true Church was a visible community of local congregations. The members of these local holiness congregations were "regenerated" and "going on to perfection." He rejected hierarchical ecclesiastical governmental structure and argued that local churches were to be independent and governed by local elders and deacons who were called by Christ from among the congregation.

---

57. Richard T. Hughes, ed., *The American Quest for the Primitive Church* (Urbana: University of Illinois Press, 1988) 125.

58. B. F. Lawrence, *The Apostolic Faith Restored* (St. Louis: Gospel, 1961) 12.

59. John P. Brooks, *The Divine Church* (Columbia, MO: Herald, 1891) 283. Brooks was convinced that authentic salvation with a desire to pursue holiness and a return to the New Testament doctrine and polity was all that was needed to bring unity and perfection among all true Christians. The Pentecostals believed that unity and perfection would come as a result of the latter rain outpouring.

Brooks made some important arguments that were later echoed throughout early Pentecostal literature. He also reflected the mindset of those who circulated among the Holiness groups. Brooks believed that the New Testament contained all the information necessary for Christian belief and polity. He was also convinced that the sanctified Christian lifestyle, rooted in love, would eradicate all selfish and sinful interests, which had created sectarianism, denominationalism, and creedalism. The power of the Holy Spirit enabled one to live a sanctified life, which ultimately would bring about unity among all true sanctified Christians.

Brooks argued that the whole New Testament was "the statute book of the Church." No new polity was needed for the Church, only a return to the God-inspired account.[60] The Reformation brought about a restoration of doctrine but failed to recover "the primitive polity and order of the Church which had been hidden, since the creation of hierarchy, in oblivion of centuries."[61] Brooks advocated that real Christians must withdraw from all forms of human-made organizational Christianity and band together in local congregations in order to form the authentic Church, which must be patterned after the true Church as revealed in the New Testament. The primitive Church of the New Testament was intended by God to be "permanent and perpetual." He stated:

> [The Church of the New Covenant] must continue the same, in oneness of faith, of order, of sacraments, of polity, till Christ should come again. These must abide unchanged, to preserve the identity of the Church. To change the one faith of the Church, or its order, or its sacraments, or its polity would be an innovation on its constitution, and it would no longer be the Church that Christ founded.[62]

Brooks was a "primitivist."[63] Like all primitivists, he desired to return to the pure Church of the New Testament era. For Brooks, the present Church was perverted and apostate. Like other restorationalists, he had to transcend at least eighteen hundred years of Christian history in order

---

60. Ibid., 26–28

61. Ibid., 39.

62. Ibid., 17.

63. Richard T. Hughes states that "the common thread that bound all primitivists together was a mutual striving to live and move in a perfect church, patterned after an apostolic model," in *The American Quest for the Primitive Church* (Urbana: University of Illinois Press, 1988) 214–15.

to discover the pure, primitive or true Church. The Wesleyan Holiness traditions resonate with primitivistic concepts of the Church.[64]

Primitivists were keenly aware of the differences between the primitive Church of Scripture and the Church of history. Brooks simply argued that the great "dissimilarity" was caused by the apostasy of the patristic Church, which was epitomized by the Roman Catholic Church. It was seen as the mother of all sectarian churches, which had fallen into complete apostasy through the Emperor Constantine. As a result, "the true Church dropped out of sight, and what remained was apostate ecclesiasticism."[65] The true Church began to resurface again as a result of the Reformation and could clearly be seen among the independent Holiness churches.

Brooks argued that the apostasy of the early Church caused the cessation of divine miracles. He did not believe that God desired to have the miracles cease with the death of the apostles; instead, he argued that the divine power of God would be manifested within the true Church and that one should not expect to see miracles in the apostate Church. God's approval had been withdrawn from the apostate Church but not permanently removed.

> The truth is that the marks of supernaturalism with which the church was originally clothed were intended to abide with it and to accredit its doctrine as Divine, just as Christ's own doctrine was accredited as Divine. As already observed, the ministry of the church was to be a continuation of the ministry of Christ, and within his design, no doubt, was to be accompanied with the same phenomena of supernaturalism that verified his own ministry. . . . And, as in the future that Church (the true Church) shall more and more emerge into notice from amidst the confusions and carnalities of sectarian Christendom, it cannot be doubted that there will be a reassertion of all the original gifts of which it was in the beginning made the possessor by its divine Lord, the gift of miracles included.[66]

Brooks's arguments help set the stage for the expectation of the restoration of the charismatic gifts to a holy community.

64. See Steven L. Ware, "Restoring the New Testament Church: Varieties of Restorationism in the Radical Holiness Movement of the Late Nineteenth and Early Twentieth Centuries," *PNEUMA* 21 (1999) 238–47.

65 Brooks, *Divine Church*, 219ff., 225.

66. Ibid., 21.

Brooks—like other prominent Holiness non-cessationists, notably A. B. Simpson—provided the Pentecostals with a powerful argument for the acceptance and validity of their movement. The manifestation of the gifts among the Pentecostals should be understood as a divine sign of the movement's legitimacy. The Pentecostals claimed that their movement ushered in the latter rain era, which the Holiness non-cessationist movements were anticipating. Hence, the latter rain motif functioned as a plot line of the Pentecostal story. The following statement by B. F. Lawrence reveals the importance that primitivism and the latter rain motif had upon Pentecostal identity:

> The honest-hearted thinking men and women of this great movement, have made it their endeavor to return to the faith and practice of our brethren who serve God prior to the apostasy. They have made the New Testament their rule of life. This effort, which is so general throughout the movement, has had a particular effect upon those who were exercised thereby. . . . The Pentecostal movement has no such history; it leaps the intervening years crying, "*Back to Pentecost*." In the minds of these honest-hearted, thinking men and women, this work of God is immediately connected with the work of God in the New Testament days. Built by the same hand, upon the same foundation of the apostles and prophets, after the same pattern, according to the same covenant, they too are a habitation of God through the Spirit. They do not recognize a doctrine or custom as authoritative unless it can be traced to that primal source of church instructions, the Lord and his apostles.[67]

Hence the validity of the Pentecostal community's existence was based upon the interpretation of Scripture. Not only was there biblical support for their existence, but the community was also being divinely approved. God was confirming to the world that the Pentecostal Christians were the fulfillment of the anticipated latter rain. The Pentecostals had the testimony of miracles to confirm their claim.

The Apostolic Faith, under the bold heading "The Promised Latter Rain Now Being Poured Out on God's Humble People," stated that,

> All along the ages men have been preaching a partial Gospel. A part of the Gospel remained when the world went into the dark ages. God has from time to time risen up men to bring back the truth to the church. He rose up Luther to bring back to the world

---

67. Lawrence, *Apostolic Faith Restored*, 11–12.

the doctrine of justification by faith. He rose up another reformer in John Wesley to establish Bible holiness in the church. Then he rose up Dr. Cullis who brought back the wonderful doctrine of divine healing. Now He is bringing back the Pentecostal Baptism to the Church.[68]

The focal point of the latter rain was the "restoration of the Gospel," but the primary character of the story was Jesus. The doctrines being restored, the fivefold Gospel, all have to do with one's understanding of the ministry of Jesus—a soteriological and ecclesiastical concern. The Pentecostal community was a continuation of the ministry of Jesus made possible by the powerful presence of the Holy Spirit in their midst.

In sum, the Pentecostals, who had been shaped by the Holiness culture of Come-outism, read Scripture without the need to appeal to the development of tradition beyond the New Testament. The unadulterated Christian history was recorded in the Acts of the Apostles. There was little need to trace a historical account of the activity of the supernatural gifts throughout Church history. Pentecostals, however, needing to present a plausible reason for the lack of supernatural manifestations, simply adopted and represented an already acceptable solution. The gifts had generally ceased due to the great apostasy of the Church; however, the gifts would be restored to those Holiness Christian communities that sought the empowerment of the Holy Spirit.[69] The arguments of Come-outism, as woven into the latter rain motif, helped to create the Pentecostal story.

Mark Noll writes, "When studying biblical primitivism, it does seem important to ask which part of the Bible functions as the standard, for it is rarely the entire text."[70] For Pentecostals, the standard was the Book of Acts. They read the whole of Scripture through the Book of Acts as if they were looking forward and backward simultaneously. Therefore, Acts served as their beginning and ending point in the development of bibli-

---

68. (Los Angeles, 1906, vol. 1, number 2, p. 1, lead article). See also Faupel, *Everlasting Gospel*, who argues that this pattern is found repeatedly in Pentecostal literature and presents a partial listing (38 n. 52).

69. Richard Hughes aptly explains the primitivistic quest of the Pentecostals. "[T]he Holiness tradition emphasized an *ethical primitivism*, concerned with a sanctified way of life, the Pentecostals sought an *experiential primitivism* directed toward recovery of the apostolic gifts of the Spirit, especially glossolalia and healing. Indeed, Pentecostals sought nothing less than a restoration of the Jerusalem Pentecost . . ." in *American Quest for the Primitive Church*, 243.

70. Ibid., 121.

cal doctrines. Donald Dayton's comment that Pentecostals read Scripture "through Lukan eyes especially with the lens of Acts" correctly captures this reality.[71] Implicit in their interpretation of the relation between the Old and New Testament, however, was the important notion that the ministry of Jesus and his community was the fulfillment of Old Testament prophetic promises.

Acts was the authentically inspired historical record of the "primitive Church." The Pentecostals compared their contemporary Christianity with the original "apostolic" pattern in Acts, and found contemporary Christianity lacking in both power and purity. They sought to continue the restoration of doctrine and practice started by the Protestant Reformers. The Pentecostals, unlike the Reformers but similar to the Holiness non-cessationist primitivists, sought the restoration of miracles. The Pentecostals, along with the Wesleyan Holiness community, embraced the Book of Acts as the normative expression of authentic Christianity.[72]

THE PENTECOSTAL STORY AND THE CENTRAL NARRATIVE CONVICTIONS OF THE COMMUNITY

The purpose of this section is to articulate the story of the first generation of Pentecostals and the central narrative convictions of that unique story. The central narrative convictions are those convictions that arise out of the story and are central to the story.[73] The central narrative convictions

71. Dayton, *Theological Roots of Pentecostalism*, 23.

72. Donald Dayton, "Asa Mahan and the Development of American Holiness Theology," *The Wesleyan Theological Journal* 9 (1974) 60–69, shows how the Book of Acts became very important in the latter period of the Holiness movements. This was due to the influence of Asa Mahan, especially his book titled *The Baptism of the Holy Ghost* which signaled an important shift in the language and theological emphasis to the book of Acts (Pentecostal themes).

73. For an insightful discussion concerning "Foundational Narrative Convictions" as they relate to hermeneutical communities see Douglas Jacobsen's "Pentecostal Hermeneutics in Comparative Perspective," a paper presented to the Annual Meeting of the Society for Pentecostal Studies, March 13–15, 1997 (Oakland, CA). Jacobsen identifies what he perceives to be *the* foundational narrative convictions of Pentecostalism as "God is doing a new thing through us" and this is different from anything that has happened before in history. Underlining these convictions is a confidence that permeates everything Pentecostals do. I disagree with Jacobsen's foundational narrative convictions but I agree that Pentecostalism articulates a bold confidence in God. This confidence is not so much a new thing as it is a restored "latter rain" that is greater than the "former rain." I will demonstrate that the central narrative convictions of the (early) Pentecostals are (was) the Fivefold Gospel made relevant through the latter rain story.

are key theological concepts inherent in the Pentecostal story, which is dramatically articulated through the proclamation of the Fivefold (Full) Gospel.

The Pentecostal story explains why the Pentecostal community exists, who they are as a community, what responsibilities they should perform, and how they fit into the larger scheme of Christian history. It shades perceptions that color and make meaningful the reading of Scripture as well as experienced reality. The story cannot be reduced to static presuppositions. The coherent story is more than a rational cognitive grid (such as presuppositions seem to suggest), which means that it cannot be removed or laid aside. It may be modified or changed but it cannot be set aside.

Douglas Jacobsen hints at this dialectical interactive epistemological process of the interpreter rooted in a hermeneutical community and the reading of Scripture. He writes:

> Our communally different readings of the Bible have largely been derived from the text [Scripture]. Our different experiences have shaped the way we see the text and situate the text in relation to ourselves and the world, but our readings of the Bible have also helped form those very experiences, helped form our foundational views of life.[74]

Every Christian tradition has a story that shapes, influences, and in some aspects determines the "meaning" of the biblical passage. The community story gives the readers a particular angle from which they see the Bible as whole. The story constructed out of Scripture will also indicate what passages in the Bible will function as a canon within the canon.

The Pentecostal story operates within the socio-cultural Pentecostal worldview and holds its central assumptions and beliefs together in a coherent and cohesive manner.[75] The story has always been the primary

---

74. Jacobsen, "Pentecostal Hermeneutics in Comparative Perspective," 5. Jacobsen lists and briefly describes ten distinguishable elements that he believes apply to all biblical hermeneuts. They are: Experience, Inherited Interpretive Schemes, Intuition, Systematic Analysis, Communal Corroboration, Reader-Response "Expansion" of the Text, Ritual Response, Desired Result, Academic Analysis and a Second Naïveté, see 2–4, for a fuller discussion. Hermeneutics is much more then adopting a certain exegetical approach.

75. Charles Kraft, *Anthropology for Christian Witness* (Maryknoll, NY: Orbis, 1996). Kraft defines a worldview "as the culturally structured assumptions, and commitments/ allegiances underlining a people's perception of reality and their response to those perceptions," 52.

The latter rain motif provided the early Pentecostals with an experiential conceptual framework and also enabled them to explain their movement convincingly. It provided the hermeneutical lens for the interpretation of Scripture and their present experience of reality.

> The early rain came at Pentecost, and immediately the seed which Jesus and His disciples had sown sprang up. This early rain continued for more than a hundred years, during which time the church was kept inundated with mighty floods of salvation. But when the church became popular and was formed into a great hierarchy, the long drought began, interspersed with a local shower of gracious revival now and then through the Middle Ages. Under the reformations, the latter rain began to be foreshadowed. The holiness revivals which have been going on in our land for the last few years are the preliminary showers of this rain. They have been glorious and wonderful: so much so that many have taken them for the latter rain itself. But we know that these revivals, though gracious, have fallen short of the apostolic revivals—the early rain. The Scriptures seem to teach that the latter rain is to be far greater than the former. . . . The early rain began on the Day of Pentecost, and the first manifestation was speaking with other tongues as the Spirit gave utterance, and then followed the healing of the sick, casting out devils, etc. So it would only be natural that the latter rain Pentecost should be repeated and followed by the same manifestation. [The latter rain] seems to have its starting point in the year 1906 in Los Angeles, Cal.[80]

The Pentecostal story was transmitted orally and through publications. Taylor's explanation of the latter rain is typical and can represent the Pentecostal story.

Like all stories, the Pentecostal story has a beginning, middle, and end. In the beginning, God poured his Spirit out on a saved and sanctified Christian community with the biblical sign of speaking in tongues (Acts 2). The Church started out pure and unified. After the death of the apostles, however, the world became more influential upon the Christian communities. The deathblow would be the conversion of Constantine, which triggered the rapid apostasy of Christianity. As a result of wandering from the truth and practice of Jesus and the apostles, the early Church would become an apostate church. The rains, which fell upon the New Testament apostolic church, began to wane.

80. Taylor, *Spirit and the Bride*, 90–91.

hermeneutical filter used to sift the Scriptures for theological meaning. It is the hermeneutical foil in which meaning is produced.

J. Richard Middleton and Brian Walsh suggest that "worldviews give faith answers to a set of ultimate grounding questions."[76] They argue that such questions could be framed as:

> (1) *Where are we?* or What is the nature of the reality in which we find ourselves? (2) *Who are we?* or What is the nature and task of human beings? (3) *What's wrong?* or How do we understand and account for the evil and brokenness? (4) *What's the remedy?* or How do we find a path through our brokenness to wholeness.[77]

The Pentecostal story performs a similar function in that it provides meaningful answers to these ultimate questions.

The story also serves as the Pentecostal version of Christianity. Hence, by identifying the Pentecostal narrative tradition, we simultaneously recognize the important contribution of the social location of the reader in her community.[78] Biblical hermeneutics is concerned with the historical horizon of Scripture but also with the equally challenging horizon of the contemporary reader.

Elsewhere I have shown how the first generation of Pentecostals interpreted Scripture with methods similar to those used by both the non cessationist Holiness community and, to some extent, the cessationist dispensational fundamentalist community.[79] Pentecostals used typology, inductive reasoning, and even dispensational schemes. Yet, what distinguished the early Pentecostal hermeneutic from that of their Holiness sisters was the distinct narrative that held these similar methods together. This distinct story encouraged them to interpret Scripture from a new angle. They were the marginalized people of the latter rain.

76. *The Transforming Vision: Shaping A Christian World View* (Downers Grove, InterVarsity, 1984) see chapter 2.

77. Middleton and Walsh, *Truth Is Stranger Than It Used To Be: Biblical Faith In Postmodern Age* (Downers Grove, IL: InterVarsity, 1995) 11.

78. I am purposefully using "her" in order to remind the readers that it was a woman who first spoke in tongues at Parham's Bible school in Topeka, Kansas and that woman played a significant role in carrying the Pentecostal message throughout the world. And it was black sanctified women who made significant contributions to the Azusa Street revival and Pentecostalism in general; see Cheryl J. Sanders, *Saints In Exile:The Holiness-Pentecostal Experience in African American Religion and Culture* (New York: Oxford University Press, 1996).

79. See footnote 12 above.

The middle of the story begins when the church embraced the Roman Empire (Constantine's granting of equal religious status to Christianity through the Edict of Milan). Consequently, God withdrew his Spirit from the apostate hierarchical Roman Church. This was the beginning of the so-called Dark Ages. The rains had stopped. During the long drought of the Middle Ages, however, the living God always had a faithful persecuted remnant. The persecuted remnant was made up of the faithful followers of Jesus Christ. Through John Wesley and the Holiness revivals, the Reformers were preparing the faithful remnant of the Church for the restoration of the promised latter rain. This brought the middle section of the story to a close. The occasional sprinkles that came during the drought, which grew more intense yet still sporadic toward the end of the drought, created a sense of anticipation that the rains were going to fall again, just as promised.

The latter rain Pentecostal outpouring was the beginning of the end of the all-encompassing dramatic Pentecostal story. Jesus was coming very soon—before their generation would die—to bring fallen human history to an end. Only the ones who were saved and "baptized with the Holy Ghost" with the biblical evidence of tongues, and who retained the sanctifying work of the Spirit manifesting divine love, would escape the great Day of Judgment coming upon the world. Thus, one needed to experience the latter rain Pentecost in order to be included among the "sealed bride of Jesus." The latter rain began to fall and it became a torrential downpour.

In conclusion, the Pentecostal story was teleological in that it brought the beginning and end of the church age together. The story affirms the past by holding onto the hope of the future through the present participatory promise of Spirit baptism. The Pentecostal story enabled Pentecostals to eclipse modernity and return to a premodern era in which the supernatural was normal, not abnormal. The Pentecostal story brought together the restoration of charismatic gifts with the imminence of the Second Coming. This narrated hermeneutical approach had a cohesive theological structure and centered upon the restorative dramatic story of God's passion for humanity. The Pentecostal story contributed to and placed constraints upon their interpretive creativity. This narrative was central to Pentecostal identity and spirituality and not only served as the primary filter through which Scripture was sifted for meaning, but was also used to interpret their experience of reality and their understanding of Christian history.

When Pentecostals read Scripture, they do so from within their cultural-contextual worldview. They read Scripture as the marginalized people of the latter rain. At the center of the dramatic narrative is Jesus, the divine-human Messiah. Jesus is a mighty miracle worker empowered by the Holy Spirit. The Fivefold Gospel, then, is the central narrative convictions of one's salvific relationship with the living God. The Pentecostal salvific relationship with Jesus is the controlling theological center. Thus, the latter rain motif cohesively holds together the restoration of the Full Gospel message and reinforces the significance of the signs and wonders within the Pentecostal community. Pentecostals are concerned to be living in continuity with the past "apostolic Christians" while existing presently as the "eschatological bride of Christ."

The analogy of a spider's web may present a better picture of how the story holds together as a cohesive interpretive narrative. At the center of the web is Jesus, with emphasis placed upon the restoration of the supernatural gifts to the pure or holy community. Coming out of the center of the web are five stabilizing theological strands identified as the Full or Fivefold Gospel, which serves as central narrative convictions of the community.[81] The outer circumference of the web is the latter rain motif, which was the common frame of reference of early Pentecostalism. Woven into this web are testimonies, experiences, and scriptural passages, all of which serve to strengthen the whole web, which is the story.[82] Therefore, what is unique to Pentecostalism cannot be reduced to a novel method or one particular doctrine. What is unique is the story that creates a living theological tradition—Pentecostalism.

81. I realize that sanctification may not be a stated cardinal doctrine of those influenced by Finished Work, however holiness of life remains an important aspect of all Pentecostal groups.

82. Even though there exists some theological differences among the Pentecostal groups, which no doubt add a distinct "regional" accent to the general Pentecostal story, it does not substantially change the structure of the story. See Faupel, *Everlasting Gospel*, chapter two for thorough overview of the early Pentecostal message.

3

Jesus the Spirit Baptizer

Signifier of a Pentecostal Narrative Theology[1]

HISTORICALLY AND THEOLOGICALLY, EARLY Pentecostal identity emerged from the early twentieth century Holiness community's reading of Acts 2. This particular biblical story which depicts the disciples' experience of receiving the gift of the Father (Spirit baptism) was and still is Pentecostals' entrance point into the biblical meta-narrative. Pentecostals read Scripture from this particular location.[2] The narrative of Acts 2, along with the experience of Spirit baptism initially evidenced with tongues moved certain Holiness communities to reconfigure their theological beliefs concerning their understanding of the mission of Jesus. As a

---

1. An earlier draft of this paper was presented at the Society for Pentecostal Studies, 2008, titled "Marks of a Wesleyan Pentecostal theology." Concerning the SPS paper, I am particularly grateful for the helpful comments raised by Mark Cartledge.

2. The importance of Acts 2 is further exemplified in the second major theological crisis of early Pentecostalism. The result becomes a clear division of Oneness and Trinitarian Pentecostals. The crisis began initially with the understanding of the precise scriptural formula for a "proper" water baptism; however, the Oneness tradition significantly truncates the early Pentecostal understandings of the doctrines of God and soteriology. For Oneness Pentecostals, Acts 2:38 becomes the Gospel in miniature. Their understanding of the doctrine of God is that God is one essence and one person. Soteriology becomes three phases of one experience: repentance, water baptism and Spirit baptism. Furthermore, the Oneness theological view called for Trinitarian Pentecostals to articulate their understanding in written doctrinal statements. For further explanation of Oneness, see David A. Reed, *In the Name of Jesus: The History and Beliefs of Oneness Pentecostals* (Blandford Forum, UK: Deo, 2008); Gregory A. Boyd, *Oneness Pentecostals and The Trinity: A worldwide movement assessed by a former Oneness Pentecostal* (Grand Rapids: Baker, 1992); and from a Oneness perspective see, David K. Bernard, *Understanding God's Word: An Apostolic Approach to Interpreting the Bible* (Hazelwood, MO: Word Aflame, 2005) 76 and Talmadge L. French, *Our God Is One: The Story of the Oneness Pentecostals* (Indianapolis: Voice & Vision, 1999).

result, the Fourfold Gospel (Jesus is Savior, Sanctifier, Healer, and Coming King) gave way to the Fivefold Gospel in light of the additional, missional activity of Jesus as the Spirit Baptizer. The Fivefold Gospel became the central narrative convictions of the earliest Pentecostal community.[3]

The book of Acts serves as the entrance into and signifier of a Pentecostal theology. Without Luke's narrative of the prophetic promise of the gift of the Father and Acts 2 as serving as initial fulfillment of such promise, the Pentecostal community most likely would not have been birthed. Pentecostals saw themselves as part of the restoration of New Testament Christianity. They were the fulfillment of past biblical prophecy of the "latter rain outpouring."God was doing a "new thing" in continuity with past biblical prophecy.[4]

In the following I will integrate the more prominent "themes" of a Pentecostal theology into three interrelated theological categories (Social Trinity, Synergistic Soteriology, and Ecclesiology) via Acts 2. Spirit baptism, with a biblical sign (tongues), is an experiential-linguistic experience from which the themes emerge. By integrating the themes into the major doctrines in a narrative fashion, I will demonstrate the significance of Spirit baptism as the initial signifier and lynch-pin of a Pentecostal theology of the Fivefold Gospel. Spirit baptism, understood as a subsequent experience to regeneration, is an essential doctrine of Pentecostal theology and should not be reduced to just a doctrine added onto the traditional forms of Evangelical theology.[5] Spirit baptism, intimately affirmed through the worshipful confession that "Jesus is the Spirit Baptizer," is the lynch-pin of Pentecostal spirituality-theology; hence I will enter the discussion through the doorway of Acts 2.[6]

---

3. The historical and theological rationale for this summary paragraph can be found in Kenneth J. Archer, *A Pentecostal Hermeneutic: Spirit, Scripture and Community* (Cleveland, TN: CPT, 2009).

4. See chapter 2.

5. I include "Wesleyanism" in this statement. I use "Wesleyan" to signal the importance of experiential synergistic soteriology. As Randy L. Maddox in his *Responsible Grace: John Wesley's Practical Theology* (Nashville: Abingdon, 1994) has demonstrated, a Wesleyan understanding of Christianity calls for a "responsible grace." "Without God's grace we *cannot* be saved; while without our grace-empowered, uncoerced participation, God's grace *will not* save" (19). Pentecostal theology will breach any previously existing Christian tradition because Pentecostal theology is its own theological tradition.

6. When Spirit baptism is removed from Pentecostal *theology*, Pentecostal *spirituality* ceases to be *Pentecostal*.

I will begin by briefly reviewing the early Pentecostal understanding of the Baptism in the Holy Spirit in order to lift up key theological themes of a Wesleyan Pentecostal theology. I will integrate the themes into the fabric of the doctrines of Trinity, Soteriology and Ecclesiology, all of which are implicitly expressed in Acts 1–2.[7]

The early Pentecostal understanding of Spirit baptism as an experience subsequent to regeneration and evidenced in other tongues was based upon their exegetical reading of the Lukan narrative—in particular Luke 24:49; Acts 1:8; 2:4, 38; 10:46; and 19:6.[8] Spirit baptism was understood to be a normal experience of salvation for those living in the last days of the latter rain. Spirit baptism was a prophetic fulfillment of an ancient promise made to God's people that God would pour out the Spirit upon all flesh. The Spirit empowered the community for witness and enabled the community to enter into deeper expressions of worship. Early Pentecostal spirituality was developing a distinct experiential theological tradition which was shaped christologically, grounded pneumatologically, and oriented eschatologically.[9]

The early spirituality of the Pentecostal communities generated distinguishable theological themes which have been identified by various scholars. Pentecostal theology is a theology of worship and witness because Pentecostal spirituality is a "passion for the Kingdom."[10] The whole

7. By paying close attention to the biblical narrative, I also will implicitly challenge the reductionist nature of Oneness theology concerning the doctrine of God and Soteriology.

8 For a more detailed discussion see Kenneth J. Archer, *A Pentecostal Hermeneutic for the Twenty-First Century,* 72–82.

9 For the most recent Pentecostal theologies that ground theology pneumatologically, see Amos Yong, *The Spirit Poured Out on All Flesh: Pentecostalism and the Possibility of Global Theology* (Grand Rapids: Baker Academic, 2005) and Frank D. Macchia, *Baptized in the Spirit: A Global Pentecostal Theology* (Grand Rapids: Zondervan, 2006). Macchia's work uses Spirit baptism as an eschatological baptism of divine love as his organizing principle of his Pentecostal theology (11–18). An excellent charismatic forerunner that reassesses Christian doctrine by grounding it pneumatological is Clark H. Pinnock, *The Flame of Love: A Theology of the Holy Spirit* (Downers Grove, IL: InterVarsity, 1996). For a historically informed and theologically rich affirmation of the significance of pneumatology for Christian life and doctrine, see charismatic Catholic theologian Killian McDonnell, *The Other Hand of God: The Holy Spirit as the Universal Touch and Goal* (Collegeville, MN: Liturgical, 2003).

10. Steven J. Land, *Pentecostal Spirituality: A Passion for the Kingdom* (Sheffield, UK: Sheffield Academic, 1993) argues that Pentecostal spirituality is a distinct lived experience in the Spirit of God and should be the starting and ongoing contributing aspect of a Pentecostal theology.

Gospel for a whole people—a "material soteriology"[11]—is the storyline of a Pentecostal theology.[12] The crown jewel of Pentecostalism is Spirit baptism as signified to the community through ecstatic speech (glossolalia).[13] One can see that the doxological confessions of the Fivefold Gospel articulated an implicit theology which can serve as the organizational centerpiece of a contemporary narrative Pentecostal theology.[14] Pentecostal spirituality is lived out in community, therefore Pentecostal theology must be an integration of *orthopistis* (right belief), *orthopathos* (holy affection), and *orthopraxis* (obedient practice). *Orthopathos* will serve as the interlocutor between *orthopraxis* and *orthopistis* because Pentecostal spirituality manifests as a passionate love for God and compassionate care for people.[15] The result of the convergence of these themes is a relational theology of *orthodoxy* (right worship) and *orthomartus* (right witness).

THE CHARACTER AND CONCERN OF THE BIBLICAL STORY: TRINITY AND SOTERIOLOGY

Pentecostal theology will be shaped by the biblical story of the Protestant canon. However, the scriptural story will be entered into via the Lukan narrative, and in particular, Acts 2:1–4. In order to make my argument that Spirit baptism signifies the above stated themes, it will be helpful to

11. See Miroslav Volf, "Materiality of Salvation: An Investigation in the Soteriologies of Liberation and Pentecostal Theologies," *Journal of Ecumenical Studies* 26 (1989) 447–67. Volf argues that Pentecostalism's soteriology, like Liberation theology is a "*materiality of salvation*" (his italics). He writes, "Salvation is not merely a spiritual reality touching only an individual person's inner being but also has to do with *bodily* human existence" which is an essential understanding of Pentecostal and Liberation soteriologies, p. 448.

12. From my perspective, the Fivefold (Full) Gospel will serve as the integrative center of a narrative Pentecostal theology. Minimally, the Gospel will serve as one uniting theme of all Pentecostal theologies. I agree with Amos Yong, *The Spirit Poured Out on All Flesh: Pentecostalism and the Possibility of Global Theology* (Grand Rapids: Baker Academic, 2005) 81–120, who sees soteriology as "the beginning thematic locus of any world Pentecostal theology" (81) and Edmund Rybarczyk, *Beyond Salvation: Eastern Orthodoxy and Classical Pentecostalism on Becoming Like Christ* (Milton Keynes, UK: Paternoster, 2004) 16, where he claims that "theology is always soteriological" for Orthodoxy and Pentecostalism. I am indebted to Dale Coulter for pointing out these references.

13. Frank Macchia, "The Kingdom and the Power: Spirit Baptism in Pentecostal and Ecumenical Perspective," in *The Work of the Spirit: Pneumatology and Pentecostalism*, ed. Michael Welker (Grand Rapids: Eerdmans, 2006) 109–25, esp. 110.

14. See chapter 1.

15. Samuel Solivan, *Spirit, Pathos and Liberation: Toward an Hispanic Pentecostal Theology* (Sheffield, UK: Sheffield Academic, 1998).

return to Acts 2:1–47. This passage is the most important biblical passage for Pentecostal spirituality, identity, and mission.

> (Acts 2:1) When the day of Pentecost had come, they were all to-gether in one place. (2) And suddenly from heaven there came a sound like the rush of a violent wind, and it filled the entire house where they were sitting. (3) Divided tongues, as of fire, appeared among them, and a tongue rested on each of them. (4) All of them were filled with the Holy Spirit and began to speak in other languages, as the Spirit gave them ability. . . . (11) . . . in our own languages we hear them speaking about God's deeds of power. ". . . (17) 'In the last days it will be, God declares, that I will pour out my Spirit upon all flesh, and your sons and your daughters shall prophesy, and your young men shall see visions, and your old men shall dream dreams. (18) Even upon my slaves, both men and women, in those days I will pour out my Spirit; and they shall prophesy. . . . (21) Then everyone who calls on the name of the Lord shall be saved.' . . . (22) . . . Jesus of Nazareth, a man attested to you by God with deeds of power, wonders, and signs that God did through him among you. (32) This Jesus God raised up, and of that all of us are witnesses. (33) Being therefore exalted at the right hand of God, and having received from the Father the promise of the Holy Spirit, he has poured out this that you both see and hear. . . . (38) Peter said to them, "Repent, and be baptized every one of you in the name of Jesus Christ so that your sins may be forgiven; and you will receive the gift of the Holy Spirit. (39) For the promise is for you, for your children, and for all who are far away, everyone whom the Lord our God calls to him." . . . (43) . . . many wonders and signs were being done by the apostles. (44) All who believed were together and had all things in common. . . . (46) Day by day, as they spent much time together in the temple, they broke bread at home and ate their food with glad and generous hearts, (47) prais-ing God and having the goodwill of all the people. And day by day the Lord added to their number those who were being saved.[16]

By starting with Pentecostals' primary biblical passage of experi-ential identity, we enter into the overarching biblical story from a Lukan perspective.[17] Theological themes contained in Scripture come into view as present communities read the landscape of Scripture. Certain themes

---

16. Unless otherwise noted all Scripture quotations are from the NRSV.

17. I am convinced that many of the themes of a Pentecostal theology are both overt and implicit in the Lukan narrative. The themes are not limited to Lukan narrative.

of Scripture emerge from the landscape because of the different social, political, and economic locations of the readers.[18] The landscape is somewhat linguistically stable and, thus, projects a consistent view for all readers. But, present readers do not view the landscape from the same location. Furthermore, readers are necessary in order to complete the communicative event, hence producing meaning. As readers, the community brings its experiential-spiritual formation which includes hearing the Spirit both through sacred Scripture and, also, through the experiences of the community with the Holy Spirit. The community dialogically engages the Scripture as it discerns the signs and voice of the Spirit.[19]

The overarching story of Scripture is about the Social Trinity's relationship with creation, particularly humanity. God exists in differentiated personhood—a loving relational community.[20] Communal loving relationality is the essential attribute of God's very being.[21]

Soteriology is the story line of the Bible. God's creative-redemptive activity is narrated through Scripture, thus our understanding of God is shaped narratively, and our experience of conversion is the entrance into the body of Christ. Soteriology, theology proper (in the sense of the doctrine of God), and community are constantly interwoven in the overarching narrative of Scripture.

We are shaped by the formative power of the biblical narrative as a primary means of mediating the revelatory activity of God to humanity. Proclamation of the Gospel of God elicits a real encounter with the Social Trinity; hence, spiritual formation begins with God's initiating revelatory encounter. Besides the ongoing relationship we have with God through the Spirit, Christian spirituality is formed through the storied world of

18. See Justo L. González, *Santa Bíblia: The Bible through Hispanic Eyes* (Nashville: Abingdon, 1996) 11–30, 18. He uses the imagery of "landscape."

19. For more detailed discussion of the roles of the Community, Holy Spirit and Scripture, see, Kenneth J. Archer, " *A Pentecostal Hermeneutic: Spirit, Scripture and Community* (Cleveland, TN: CPT, 2009) chapter 6, and Robby Waddell, *The Spirit of the Book of Revelation* (Dorset, UK: Deo, 2006) 39–96.

20. See Catherine M. LaCugna, *God For Us: The Trinity and Christian Life* (San Francisco: HaperSanFrancisco, 1991).

21. This understanding is dismissed if God is simply one person. If the essential being of God is not dynamic relational love, then the eternal nature of God is a static monad. As Boyd correctly points out in his *Oneness Pentecostals and the Trinity*, the Oneness view of God "completely undermines the genuineness of the Father's personal love for the Son and the Son's personal love of the Father spoken so poignantly throughout the New Testament" (183).

Scripture and the testimonies of those in and outside the Christian community. Christian spirituality is inherently relational, communal, and multidimensional.

The dramatic narrative of Scripture has a beginning, middle, and end which correspond with three gracious acts of God. The first salvific act is creation; the second salvific act is redemption; and the final salvific act is glorification.[22] From the opening to the close of the biblical story, it is the Social Trinity's relational passion to have a covenant people who freely respond to God's gracious invitation to enter into intimate redemptive relationship with God, God's people, and God's creation.

The salvific act of creation not only provides the material substance *quote* for the appearance of human life, but also makes available the means for God's prevenient grace to come to humanity. Prevenient grace initiates one into the people of God and anticipates both converting grace and perfecting grace. The salvific act of redemption provides the means for conscious conversion into the body of Christ while anticipating God's perfecting grace. The future salvific act of glorification provides the means for God's perfecting grace in which creation and humanity are fully liberated and entirely restored. The reign of God has fully come! "God is the eschatological trinitarian presence who is the goal and limit of all things, so history, as God's great theater, moves *by* God *in* God *to* God."[23]

The triune God—Spirit, Father, Son—all share in the mission of creation, redemption and re-creation. The Holy Spirit is at work with the Father and the Son from the beginning—even the beginning of creation—to the completion of the glorification of creation. "When the Father sends his Word, he always sends his Breath. In their joint mission, the Spirit and Son are distinct but inseparable."[24] The Son is incarnated, the permanent visible presence of the invisible God. Jesus is the Christ—the anointed of God by the Holy Spirit. The mission of the Holy Spirit is indissolubly interwoven into the mission of Jesus, the Son of God and Messiah which is interdependent and inseparable from the mission of the Father. The mission of God is heard in the biblical refrain, "I will be their God and they will be my people."

22. See Gustavo Gutiérrez, *A Theology of Liberation: History, Politics, and Salvation* (Maryknoll, NY: Orbis, 1988) 87.

23. Steve Land, "A Passion for the Kingdom: Revisioning Pentecostal Spirituality," *Journal of Pentecostal Theology* (1992) 19–46, 29–30.

24. *Catechism of the Catholic Church* (Liguori, MO: Liguori, 1994) 181.

THE RELATIONAL OPENNESS OF THE SOCIAL TRINITY

Acts 1–2 is saturated with language associated with the persons of the Trinity. From a close reading of the Lukan narrative, the opportunity to experience Spirit baptism is a result of the Father's commitment to Jesus of Nazareth, who is the exalted Lord and Messianic prophet. "This Jesus God raised up, and of that all of us are witnesses. Being therefore exalted at the right hand of God, and having received from the Father the promise of the Holy Spirit, he has poured out this that you both see and hear" (Acts 2:32–33). The Lukan Jesus "ordered them not to leave Jerusalem, but to wait there for the promise of the Father." "This," he said, "is what you have heard from me; for John baptized with water, but you will be baptized with the Holy Spirit not many days from now."[25] The promise of the Father is the gift of the Holy Spirit. The gift of the Father, however, was not available until it was first given to Jesus. Even though the Spirit rested upon him at his water baptism it was not until after his ascension that Jesus poured out the Spirit upon the obedient followers who were waiting worshipfully in Jerusalem. Throughout the Acts narrative, Jesus continues to Spirit baptize individuals who repent and believe. Jesus as the Spirit Baptizer fulfills the testimony of John the Baptist. Jesus as Savior and Lord fulfills the prophetic promise of Joel. The Spirit is manifested to the community through the primary scriptural symbols of fire, wind, and pouring out. In fact, most of the prominent biblical symbols of the Spirit coalesce in this passage. Furthermore, the Spirit testifies of the Gospel through signs, wonders, and prophetic speech (xenolalia as well as glossolalia) in conjunction with and through the community. For those observing, the reception of Spirit baptism is signified repetitively through tongues speech.

There is one more important reference to baptism in Luke's Gospel, and this is also associated with Jesus and his ministry: "I have a baptism with which to be baptized, and what stress I am under until it is completed!" (Luke 12:50). This reference to baptism finds it places in a larger continuous discourse concerning "vigilance in the face of crises."[26] Joel Green points out that this baptism refers to the eschatological mission of Jesus Christ to create a new kinship (family) group. This means that to join the followers of Jesus requires a reorientation and transformation. To

---

25. See Luke 3:16, Matt 3:11, and Mark 1:8.

26. Joel B. Green, *The Gospel of Luke* (Grand Rapids: Eerdmans, 1997) 476.

follow Jesus means to repent and requires one to turn away from her/his natural family, which are those people who have not embraced the way of salvation. This results in division. Division is an aspect of God's judgment upon those who do not believe and creates possible persecution upon those who follow Jesus. The reference to baptism is most likely connected to Jesus' commissioning which consumes him and drives him forward.[27] Thus, it refers to Jesus' whole mission;[28] a mission which includes baptizing his followers in the Holy Spirit resulting in the re-constituting of the community as one family and commissioning them into the messianic mission of the Spirit and the Son.

The centrality of Christology in Pentecostal identity only enhances an appreciation and affirmation of the Social Trinity. To take the ministry of Jesus seriously as presented in the Gospels is to celebrate the mystery of the Trinity working for the salvation of creation, especially the redemption of humanity. God sends both the Son and the Spirit as partners in the mission of the redemption of fallen creation. The Spirit's activity in creation underlies the Spirit's activity in the redemptive work of Jesus and the missional work of the Christian community. The constitutive and reciprocating missional roles of the Spirit and the Son are grounded pneumatologically and shaped christologically resulting in a robust trinitarian theology. Jesus' ministry and the Holy Spirit's mission are interrelated without becoming indistinguishable. From this perspective we avoid the subordination of the Son to the Spirit or the Spirit to the Son by articulating the missional activity of the Spirit and Jesus in the eschatological, transformative redemption of God's creation.

Acts 2 opens with: "When the day of Pentecost had come."[29] Pentecost was one of three annual pilgrim festivals that provided opportunity for the people to offer thanksgiving for the bountiful grain harvest. Pentecost marked the end of the grain harvest (Exod 23:14).[30] The festivals were

27. See ibid., 507–11.

28. I would also include Jesus's substitutional death, yet it is not limited to his death and resurrection.

29 Pentecost refers to the Feast of Weeks, also called the Feast of First Fruits (Exod 34:22; Num 28:26; Deut 16:9–10, 16). See Stanley M. Horton, *The Book of Acts* (Springfield, MO: Gospel, 1981) 29.

30. The Feast of Booths which commemorates Israel's 40 year journey through the wilderness toward the promise land and the Passover are the other two festivals (Lev 23:34; Deut 16:13). See also Roger Stronstad, *The Prophethood of All Believers: A Study in Luke's Charismatic Theology* (Sheffield, UK: Sheffield Academic, 1999) 54–70.

closely connected to the agricultural cycle of Israel and were significant crisis points in Israel's relationship with Yahweh. They are interwoven into the historic salvation of God's chosen people. [31] Together, these festivals celebrate the themes of liberation, revelation, and covenantal journey.[32]

Pentecost is linked to the revelation of Yahweh and the giving of the commandments at Mount Sinai.[33] Yahweh's self disclosure to Moses indicates that God initiates and enters into a covenantal relationship with people. Yahweh will be their God and they will be Yahweh's people. Yahweh vulnerably enters into this covenant as Sovereign Lord who is faithful to his promises and willing to enter into solidarity with their suffering.[34] Yahweh is creator and redeemer. The people liberated by God "will become God's covenant partner in a mission to all the earth."[35] The significance of Sinai is the self disclosure of God along with the receiving of the Law and the people's willing response to faithfully obey and follow Yahweh.

---

31. Walter Brueggemann, *Reverberations of Faith: A Theological Handbook of Old Testament Themes* (Louisville: Westminster John Knox, 2002) 72–74. Significant events in Israel's historic memory are presented as replications of the exodus event, see Gen 15:7; Josh 4:23–24; 1 Sam 4:8, 6:6; Jer 21:15; Amos 9:7, pp. 72–73. See also Bruce C. Birch, Walter Brueggemann, Terence E. Fretheim, and David L. Petersen, *A Theological Introduction to the Old Testament* (Nashville: Abingdon, 1999) 99–130.

32. Brueggemann, *Reverberations of Faith*, 72. The Day of Atonement is coupled to the exodus. The exodus is the liberation of Yahweh's people out of Egyptian captivity and the triumph over the cosmic forces of chaos that threaten God's people. This historic event is paradigmatic for the people of Yahweh. The narrative account of Passover (Exodus 1–15) "begins with Israel's cry of oppression in Exod 2:23–25 and ends with Israel's song of emancipation in Exod 15:1–18." The exodus liberates the people from oppression and thrusts them forward in their journey where they eventually will come to Mount Sinai and then move towards the promise land. This journey is inherently relational and missional, for Israel is to be a light to the nations.

33. See Stronstad, *Prophethood of All Believers*, 54–70.

34. The vulnerability of God is an important quality of God's covenantal relationality with humanity and creation which opens God up to suffering. See further, Terence F. Fretheim, *The Suffering of God: An Old Testament Perspective* (Philadelphia: Fortress, 1984). According to Fretheim, there are three reasons for God's suffering: "God suffers *because* of the people who are suffering," "God suffers *with* the people who are suffering," "God suffers for the people" (108). Fretheim shows that even though God's life is affected by suffering, God nonetheless is consistent in character and "God will remain gracious and merciful and abounding in steadfast love" (124).

35. Bruce C. Birch, Walter Brueggemann, Terence E. Fretheim, and David L. Petersen, *A Theological Introduction to the Old Testament*, 110.

In Acts 2, Pentecost is a historic point in the mission of God where the very Spirit of God comes from the end of history and breaks into the present. The Spirit is poured out in order to gather up the followers of Jesus and empower them for their eschatological trinitarian mission in the world. The Spirit empowered community enters into the mission of the Spirit through the baptismal work of Jesus. The community of the Spirit is to testify to the deeds of God and confirm the Sonship of Jesus. The prophetic people proclaim the "Full" Gospel as they imitate the ministry of Christ Jesus, thus furthering the mission of the Father through the personal presence of the Spirit. The community is empowered to carry forward the mission of Christ into the entire world.[36] Tongues, miracles, visions, persecutions, and signs are an important part of the charismatic mission. This is a Pentecostal spirituality which "seeks to extend its self-understanding as the community of the Spirit *in* the world and *for* the world, but not *of* the world."[37]

The self disclosure of God involves the act of self exposure. God is revealed as liberator through Israel's exodus. Jesus is revealed as the messianic Lord through the resurrection. At Pentecost, God is revealed as the Spirit of Life. Pentecost is a definitive historic moment in the salvific journey of the people of God. Pentecost is an intimate yet "tangible" revealing of the Holy Spirit who becomes a permanent sojourner with the pilgrim people of God in the absence of the resurrected Christ.[38] The eschatological Spirit moves the community through the world towards the coming reign of God, which is and is yet to come. This revealing is the one triune God, who is Father, Son, and Spirit.

In our experience of regeneration, the Spirit baptizes us into the body of Christ; however, at Pentecost, Jesus is the one who both sends the Spirit and baptizes us into the Spirit.[39] The Spirit proceeds from the

---

36. Luke 4:18–19 plays a significant role in understanding the mission of Jesus for the Pentecostal communities.

37. Eldin Villafañe, *The Liberating Spirit: Toward an Hispanic American Pentecostal Social Ethic* (Grand Rapids: Eerdmans, 1993) 193.

38. Through the various manifested signs associated with the Spirit of God, God the Spirit is present in a visible and tangible way.

39. Stanley M. Horton correctly points out that Jesus' ascension did not end his work, see *The Book of Acts*, 16. A close reading of Horton's commentary on Acts and his *What the Bible Says About The Holy Spirit* (Springfield, MO: Gospel, 1976) demonstrates an uncomfortable fit with basic Protestant Evangelical theology and clearly rejects popular understandings of finished work theology. He does not see Pentecost as the birth of the Church because the Church was already in existence, nor does he understand Jesus' work

Father through Jesus to the community and draws the community into a new dimensional relationship with the Spirit, thus grounding the community into the relational essence of God via the ministry of Jesus. As an event, Pentecost looks back to the Passover Lamb, who makes possible the exodus for the people of God, and also looks forward to the full consummation of God's reign. The Pentecostal community is called to stand against the present evil age accomplished through active participation in the worship of the Social Trinity and holistic witness to the world in anticipatory hope of the returning Christ Jesus. Pentecost is a pivotal moment in the revealing of the Holy Spirit in the trinitarian mission for the restoration of creation.

At Pentecost, the Spirit entered into a new relationship with humanity, and humanity enters into a new relationship with God and God's creation.[40] Pentecost is a cosmic event in that it is also a foretaste of the coming liberation of creation.[41] Spirit baptism initiates the person into this cosmic struggle. The Spirit sighs with broken humanity and creation moans for the redemption of the people of God.[42] Therefore, tongues speech echoes the cries of the Spirit as lament without negating the euphoric presence of the Spirit as energizing hope. The prayerful tongues speech of the community offers praise to God that is a protest to the forces of evil.

With Liberationists, Pentecostals should affirm that there is only one historic salvation, only one sacred history. Furthermore, God's involvement within created space-time is not a secondary reality for God, but is the reality of the Social Trinity's relational activity with and in creation. Creation, then, moves forward to its final destiny, which is God.[43] The

---

to have ended—he is still Spirit baptizing his followers. Horton states, "Hebrews 9:15, 17 shows that it was the *death* of Christ that put the New Covenant into effect. From the resurrection Day when Jesus breathed on the disciples, the Church was constituted as a new covenant body" (31).

40. Pentecost brings about a *new* historic relational dimension for the community because the community now becomes the Temple of the Holy Spirit.

41. The Acts citation of Joel indicates that this event is apocalyptic and cosmic.

42. Rom 8:19, 23, 26–27.

43. God transcends all creaturely existence in the sense that God is separate from and distinct from creation, yet God is the origin, source, and ultimate goal of creation. God is infinite and self sufficient apart from creation, yet creation is dependent upon God for its very existence. The transcendence of God affirms God is "wholly other," the infinite self-sustaining One who created everything that exists. "Because God is not a finite being

Spirit, in relationship with the Father and Jesus, draws creation into the life of God while plunging the people of God into the relational fellowship of the Social Trinity.[44] The result is a new relationship—new for the people of God and new for the living God. This relationship, however, is in continuity with God's past relationship with creation and God's people, Israel, and looks forward to the consummation of creation.

The parichoretic relationship of the living God is the necessary "space" for the participatory activity of each person of the Social Trinity. Because God is a loving relationality, the persons of God open up to creation. This is a hospitable activity of God's relational love that is shared with volitional creatures. God is not a static nomad but a dynamic triune being. The activity of revelation is a risky venture for God, because God allows for creatures to reject and resist God. People even pollute God's good creation. However, God also invites humanity to enter into a covenant relationship where redemption is experienced and full liberation is promised. God's suffering is connected to God's desire to have a people who respond and cooperate with God's gracious salvation, "allowing them full opportunity to participate in shaping their own future."[45]

God comes to us from beyond. God's eschatological coming to his creation triggers the beginning of the end. God will renew all of creation which will abolish forever the distinction of heaven and earth by bringing together a new creation which includes the New Jerusalem coming down from heaven. God's dwelling place will come visibly and remain permanently with God's people. God and the Lamb will be the temple,[46] and the people are the temple of the Spirit of God.[47] We will be God's covenant people; the Social Trinity will be our God; and God will be the all in all.[48]

Pentecostal theology must tease out the relational openness of the Trinity in ways that are consistent with the community's experiences of the Spirit. Reflection upon Pentecostal spirituality in light of the biblical narrative will break the mold of classical Trinitarian views. God is loving

---

existing among other beings God is able to be incomparably present to all, closer to them than they are to themselves," (Richard Bauckham, *Theology of Revelation* [Cambridge: Cambridge University Press, 1993] 46).

44. See Macchia, "Kingdom and the Power," 125.

45. Fretheim, *Suffering of God*, 124.

46. Rev 21:22.

47. 1 Cor 6:19.

48. 1 Cor 15:28.

relationality and God, without internal necessity, opens God's being up for human participation in God's missional journey. The biblical story is the triune God's story.

SCRIPTURAL SOTERIOLOGICAL SYNERGISM

Salvation includes all the redemptive blessings of God. Salvation cannot be reduced to a static positional state of existence outside of creation, but as a reality in and for creation. Salvation must include living and moving in the Spirit—a dynamic journey with the Social Trinity in the created space-time continuum. This journey (*via salutis*) is possible because of God's salvific acts of creation and redemption in anticipation of glorification. Salvation, then, can only take place in God's created space-time continuum.[49] Furthermore, personal salvation cannot be separated from community or creation and must not be reduced to the interior salvation of the human soul. The Gospel is good news because our hope is in the resurrection from the dead. Healing is a proleptic foretaste of glorification and cannot be removed from the atonement.

Spirit baptism is a proleptic foretaste of the fulfillment of God's promise of the latter rain outpouring and as such is a redemptive blessing; hence it must be included as a vital aspect of salvation. Spirit baptism is most definitely an empowerment for the eschatological *missio Dei*. We come from God's salvific creativity and return to God through the Social Trinity's redemptive activity. Spirit baptism is an eschatological event that is connected experientially to Soteriology. This experience is distinct from initial conversion but nonetheless is sown into the very seed of God's salvific acts of creation and redemption.[50]

In Acts 2, the disciples obeyed Jesus and waited in Jerusalem. The fact that they are called disciples prior to the experience of Spirit baptism indicates that they were in a redemptive relationship with God. They were

---

49. Pentecostal soteriology cannot be reduced to simply "penal" substitutionary atonement, or initial conversion of justification. Our concept of atonement is similar to the *Christus Victor* model. It must embrace the various biblical metaphors in such a way that a rich vibrant soteriology emerges.

50. See R. Hollis Gause, *Living in the Spirit: The Way of Salvation*, rev. ed. (Cleveland, TN: CPT, 2009). Gause affirms the unitary nature of salvation while affirming a logical order of salvation as regenerated, sanctified and Spirit baptized. He argues all the redemptive seeds of salvation are sown into regeneration.

anticipating the gift of the Baptism in the Holy Spirit (Acts 1:4; 2:4). The gift of the Father was received and they spoke in tongues as the Spirit gave the ability. The wording of this passage indicates a synergistic Soteriology. A Pentecostal scriptural synergism affirms that God always initiates and, yet, calls for human response and cooperation. God does provide the enabling grace, but this grace does not determine our response. We can resist and grieve the Spirit. We are able to respond affirmatively to God's Spirit because of prevenient grace. Prevenient grace, unlike the Reformed tradition's general and effectual grace, "is a helping grace in that it restores human freedom, but is not a coercive grace" because it can be resisted.[51] Prevenient grace is God's compassionate unmerited move to humanity which enables humans to respond to the Spirit's call to salvation. We confess Jesus as Savior not because we are passive (a monergistic view), but because we are actively cooperating with the Spirit. God has initiated the relationship without determining our responses (a scriptural synergistic view). From this perspective Pentecostal spirituality-theology is marked by an experiential synergistic Soteriology.

Jesus is our Spirit Baptizer, yet we speak in tongues as the Spirit gives utterance. Glossolalia is a doxological response to the Spirit's presence in our community. We cooperate with the Spirit. The Spirit speaks through us. This speech is a free response to the revelation of God's glory—a testimony of the working of the Spirit as a witness to the Trinitarian fellowship.

Spirit baptism, justification, sanctification, healing, and glorification are all redemptive experiences of God's liberating grace. God's redemptive grace heals us from the infectious disease of sin. Redemption affects our ontological existence because it unites us with God. These redemptive manifestations are proleptic signs of God's reign, which is and is yet to come in fullness. We are gathered up, as they say, in the "Divine dance" of life. The pneumatological dimension of Spirit baptism as an ontological participation in the Social Trinity helps to further develop a robust Pentecostal synergistic Soteriology.

Spirit baptism is a normal experience, subsequent to regeneration yet sown into the very first salvific act—creation. As Blaine Charette has recently argued, Spirit baptism does indeed have something significant to

---

51. W. David Buschart, *Exploring Protestant Traditions: An Invitation to Theological Hospitality* (Downers Grove, IL: InterVarsity, 2006) 192.

contribute to the *imago Dei*.[52] Pentecost is a convergence of the mission of God with the image of God. Pentecost is not the birth of the Church but a reconstitution of the people of God into the relational mission of the Social Trinity. "The eschatological Spirit operates in the lives of believers effecting a transformation that fashions" them into the image of God "because they are being conformed to the image of Christ."[53] The empowered mission is connected to a transformed people who are imaging God—the Social Trinity. The community testifies to the grace of God as they worship the true God in relationship to one another and in relationship with the Social Trinity. [54]

This affirmation of the necessity of Spirit baptism for God's people as subsequent experience to initial conversion is a frequently cited ecumenical issue.[55] From my perspective, this is an experience that is realized in one's communal journey with God (*via salutis*), yet is an experience distinguishable from initial repentance and justification. Spirit baptism follows a logical ordering, but this logic is always swallowed up in the dynamic soteriological journey with the people of God living in the Spirit of God.[56]

The Lukan narrative connects Spirit baptism as necessary for the communities' continuation of the mission of Jesus Christ. Jesus Christ is the paradigmatic figure whom we follow through the Holy Spirit. Since

52. "Reflective Speech: Glossolalia and the Image of God," *PNEUMA* 28 (2006) 189–201.

53. Ibid., 193.

54. As LaCugna points out in *God For Us*, "The ontology of person also incorporates the central concern of Greek theology with Jesus Christ as the norm of personhood, and with the Spirit as the one who deifies us by conforming us to the person of Christ" (14, and 243–50). Soteriology is possible because humanity is an important aspect of the Trinity, in particular Christology. The incarnation is the initial point of the restoration of the image of God through the divination of humanity by the Holy Spirit.

55. There are many distinctions and theological divisions among the various Christian traditions. This, however, is particularly problematic for non-Pentecostal Evangelicals, especially from the Reformed persuasion.

56. In the NT, there is no one paradigm for the order of salvation, see Mark 1:15, Kingdom has come; repent, believe; Acts 2:38, Repent, be baptized, sins forgiven, receive Holy Spirit; Rom 10:9–17, Send, preach, hear, believe, confess, be justified and saved. In light of the argument thus far, the following questions should be raised: If Spirit baptism is not a redemptive blessing, what kind of experience is it? If it does not contribute to our fellowship with God, why should anyone seek or even expect it? If it does not open up a dimension in our relationship with the Social Trinity, why should Pentecostals proclaim it as part of the "Full" Gospel?

Jesus's personal Spirit baptism awakened him to a new dimensional relationship with the Holy Spirit, should we not expect the personal experience of the outpouring of the Spirit to awaken us to a new dimensional relationship with the Holy Spirit? I recognize that other Christian traditions present their theological understandings of Spirit baptism as an important aspect of soteriology which are inconsistent with ours.[57] This may be due to the fact that some are not taking the Lukan narrative seriously as a theological formational narrative, or, as I indicated earlier in the chapter, they may not be able to see the landscape because of their social location and theological predispositions.[58] We should not balk at being Pentecostal, nor should we dismiss Luke-Acts as highlighting Spirit baptism as such an important biblical experiential theme. Ecumenically speaking, we can be collaborative and cooperative without becoming confused as to our own identity which is primarily but, not solely, formed by the Lukan narrative, especially Acts.

Spirit baptism, like Sanctification, is not a one-time experience. Sanctification is continuous, punctiliar, and episodic because we are a pilgrim people in a dynamic relationship with God. Like Sanctification, Spirit baptism brings an initial liberation, an eruption of ecstatic speech of empowered witness and charismatic worship. However, re-fillings are an important aspect of the way of salvation. Because Spirit baptism is a seed sown into regeneration, it can become a subsequent realized redemptive benefit for both the individual in community and the community. Unlike popular views of justification, it will never be a benefit that is positional alone—simply an accredited "alien righteousness." It is a moment when one is possessed by the Spirit which generally happens as one in community is pursuing God passionately in anticipation of the reception of the gift of the Father. The Baptism in the Holy Spirit is a baptism of fire that purges and protects, propels us into mission, and plunges us into the depths of God's being. Spirit baptism is both effective and affective. Hence, we Pentecostals confess that Jesus is the Spirit Baptizer as well as Savior, Sanctifier, Healer, and Coming King.

Pentecostal theology articulates a synergistic Soteriology. Spirit baptism becomes the experiential point of convergence of the *missio Dei* and

---

57. All Christian traditions affirm the importance of Spirit baptism.

58. For example, the uneasiness that Protestants have with Acts as a formative theological narrative and that Protestant theologians often associate Spirit baptism with regeneration.

the *imago Dei*. The pneumatological dimension of Spirit baptism as an ontological participation in the Social Trinity helps to further develop a robust Pentecostal synergistic Soteriology. This understanding affirms that Jesus' ministry and the Holy Spirit's mission are interrelated without becoming indistinguishable.

PNEUMATIC MISSIONAL ECCLESIOLOGY

Acts 2 highlights the importance of a visible community that lives in the world but is not of the world. The voluntary nature of the community is captured by the followers of Jesus obeying and going to Jerusalem to wait for the gift of the Father. Further, Acts indicates that the community enters into a cooperative fellowship of mutual sharing of material necessities in order to live. The community is a visible confessing community that is charismatic in its very existence. They proclaim the good news with missionary zeal to the ends of the earth. The good news of salvation includes living as an alternative society within the world. The community exists as a contrast society *in* the world and *for* the world without being *of* the world. The community is not a product of worldly systems or existence, because at Pentecost the community is reconstituted as the body of Christ *and* the temple of the Spirit. A pneumatic ecclesiology is essential to a Pentecostal theology.

The Church is not conceived by the platonic conception of God's election in the ever-eternal past; rather, it is constituted by its future destiny as related to God's reign. In this sense it is eschatological. God's eschatological reign has already been consummated in the future by God's promise. The Spirit is drawing the present manifestation of the reign of God to its full consummation in the *eschaton*. In the process of this drawing, the focus of the present Church is to model the "glorious human fellowship—a recreation of shalom" that is to fully come at the consummation of the second coming of Christ Jesus.[59] Therefore, the Church is a sign of God's reign in the earth.[60]

The Church is within the kingdom of God, but she is not the entire kingdom. Through the Spirit, the kingdom of God far transcends the

---

59. I attribute this language to Andrew S. Hamilton, see footnote below.

60. This paragraph is the result of collaborative discussion with Andrew S. Hamilton. For further elaboration see our essay, "Anabaptism-Pietism and Pentecostalism: Scandalous Partners in Protest."

boundaries of the Church. The Church is within the kingdom in the sense that the Spirit of God reigns as the redemptive presence of God through the Church, which is the body of Christ. The Church is a result of the Spirit's work of drawing people into fellowship with God and each other through Jesus Christ. As a creation of the kingdom the mission of the Church is to proclaim and demonstrate the good news of the kingdom.[61] As such, the Church directs the attention of creation to the *eschaton.* The Church is not dissolved in the *eschaton,* but it finally realizes the promise as it participates in the liberation of creation. The glorified Church remains the "shalom of the Social Trinity." The Church as the temple of the Spirit is the radiating glory of God. The Church as the body of Christ is the particular location in the cosmos of God's tangible presence.

The Church as an "eschatological trinitarian missionary fellowship" is a communion in the Holy Spirit.[62] The Church is a communion of diversity and unity in the Spirit. The gifts and offices are distributed by the sovereignty of the Holy Spirit for the benefit of the whole body.[63] The charismatic gifts serve as signs of the eschatological presence of the living God breaking into the world. The gifts function both as edification for the local church and as redemptive "signs" to those outside the body of Christ—those who belong to the world. The gifts are an extension of the ministry of Christ to the world. The gifts enable the Church to fulfill its purpose as an eschatological missionary fellowship.

The local church is made up of faithful followers of the Lord Jesus Christ and made alive by the Holy Spirit. It is a contrast society because it is the body of Christ. As such the local church is a sacramental presence of Jesus Christ in and to the world. "The Church is the sacrament of Christ because it represents him in the world."[64] The Holy Spirit empowers the community for mission through the distribution of gifts and callings

---

61. In essence the kingdom of God was present in their midst in the person of Jesus Christ, thus where the Spirit of Christ is present, so God's kingdom is present. However, the full establishment of God's kingdom is yet to occur with the second advent of Christ. In this sense it is "not yet." We anticipate the full consummation while we participate in the real yet transitory manifestations of God's kingdom.

62. I attribute this to Steve Land. See Steven J. Land, *Pentecostal Spirituality: A Passion for the Kingdom* (Sheffield, UK: Sheffield Academic, 1993) 182–208.

63. See Land, *Pentecostal Spirituality*, 205.

64. Pinnock, *Flame of Love*, 119, 121.

upon individuals in community. In this way "the Church is an instrument of Christ, called to carry on his mission in the power of the Holy Spirit."[65]

As a contrast society, the emphasis is on the quality of the character of the Church as the body of Christ in the world. Philip D. Kenneson writes in *Beyond Sectarianism*:

> Christians should regard the world not as a separate place, but as a way of life ordered by a set of narratives, practices, and convictions that is at odds with the narratives, practices and convictions the Church is called to embody as a condition of its discipleship to Jesus Christ.[66]

The Church is a contrast society because it is animated by the Holy Spirit. The world is animated by those fallen humans and demonic spirit forces which create societal structures and institutions in opposition to the purpose and presence of the living God. The world is polluted by competing narratives in opposition to God's narrative. The Christian community, and in our case, the Pentecostal community's identity is ordered by a different story (arising out of the meta-narrative of Scripture), a different set of convictions, (which arise out of the story), and a different set of practices. The Church is to embody before the world a distinct socio-political alternative as the body of Christ. The Church as the dwelling place of the Holy Spirit is both a witness of life to a dying world and a sacred space within the world.

Pentecostal ecclesiology is a charismatic counter-culture community.[67] Witness is the responsibility of the eschatological missionary community in ministry to the world. Witness is not so much a pragmatic activity as it is an ontological existence in the world. Witness flows out of its worship of God. Witness and worship are doxological because they are reciprocal and inseparable relational privileges of the Pentecostal community as a result of entering into a redemptive relationship with the Social Trinity.[68]

65. Ibid., 116.

66. *Beyond Sectarianism: Re-Imaging Church and World* (Harrisburg, PA: Trinity, 1999) 87.

67. See Kenneth J. Archer and Andrew S. Hamilton, "Anabaptism-Pietism and Pentecostalism: Scandalous Partners in Protest," *Scottish Journal of Theology* 63:2 (2010) 185–202

68. Pentecostals hold to a relational synergistic view of salvation that is articulated by the Full Gospel. God always initiates the relationship through God's prevenient grace that

The Church as a charismatic community sees visions of Jesus Christ and manifests gifts of the Holy Spirit. These function as an extension of the local church's ministry into the world. The Church as a contrast and charismatic community is embodied by the presence of the Holy Spirit and empowered by the Holy Spirit in order to carry on the redemptive mission of our Lord Jesus Christ. The Church is to be a priesthood of all believers and a prophethood of all believers. Gifts function as redemptive signs for those outside the Church. In this sense, they serve as signs and wonders and empowerment for redemptive evangelistic purposes. Gifts function as a means of edification for the Church and individuals-in-community. Gifts are initiated by the Holy Spirit, yet, require the participation of the individual-in-community. Gifts serve as signs of the future eschatological presence of God breaking into the present fallen world, thus they have a teleological function. They point us to the end which is God. In this way, the gifts continue to manifest the compassionate care of the living God for all of creation and continue to provide opportunities of transformative healing to individuals-in-community. The healings are proleptic and testify to a material salvation—a salvation which finds its fullness in the coming reign of God.

CONCLUSION

Pentecost is a proleptic celebration of God's liberation for creation which anticipates the glorification of creation. Pentecost is a definitive event for the Church because it reconstitutes the family of God into the body of Christ and the temple of the Holy Spirit. The Social Trinity enters into a new relationship with humanity. Pentecost anticipates future outpourings of the Spirit upon the community and those coming into the community. Spirit baptism plunges us into a new relationship with God and thrusts us into the world as God's people. The intersection of the mission of God and the image of God creates an eschatological missionary fellowship. The Spirit draws us into the relational "struggle" of the Social Trinity's mission. *Glossolalia* is lament and praise to God, prayer to and with God, and protest to the world.[69] *Glossolalia* is a sign of the presence of the Spirit among the community and a foretaste of the coming reign of God.

is the result of a personal and particular revelatory encounter of the Holy Spirit.

69. The importance of the community praying cannot be overstated in Luke-Acts. Prayer is closely connected to the experience of revelation, anointing, healing, deliver-

4

Nourishment for Our Journey

The Pentecostal Via Salutis *and Sacramental Ordinances*[1]

JESUS OUR SPIRIT BAPTIZER: A PERSONAL TESTIMONY

MY SPIRIT BAPTISM EXPERIENCE took place at an Assembly of God church in the late summer of 1983.[2] I was saved in June 1983 and water baptized by immersion in July of the same year at a church fellowship. During this time period, God was getting me cleaned up. I spent much time at the altars confessing, repenting, and consecrating myself to the living God. I was calling on the living God to change me, cleanse me, and to sanctify me. Late in August, during a Sunday evening service, the pastor was passionately preaching about the importance of the Baptism in the Holy Spirit. He drew his message from passages in Acts 1 and 2. He made it clear that tongues would accompany Spirit baptism. He cautioned the congregation not to seek tongues, but, instead, worship Jesus Christ. Jesus, he assured, would fill us with the Holy Spirit. The initial biblical evidence of Spirit baptism would be manifested in tongues—a personal spiritual heavenly language that would enhance one's personal relationship with God. The pastor said, "God will not move your tongue, you must cooperate with God by surrendering it and speaking as the Spirit gives you the utterances" (Acts 2:4). The experience of Spirit baptism would empower one to be a better witness for Jesus in word, deed, and lifestyle

1. A version of this essay by the same title was presented at the 32nd Annual Meeting of the Society for Pentecostal Studies (Asbury, Kentucky), March 20–22, 2003. Special thanks go to Lester Ruth, Associate Professor of Worship and Liturgy at Asbury Theological Seminary, for his helpful response to the paper.

2. New Life AOG is located in Wellington, Ohio, and at that time averaged about 110 in attendance for Sunday morning service.

(Acts 1:8). Toward the end of the message he gave the appeal, an altar call, for those who would like to be Spirit baptized.

The pressure was building inside me during the sermon, and I could sense the presence of the living God in our midst. The invitation was given, but I was hesitant about going forward. I had already been to the altar many times. The pastor started to get irritated with us because no one was responding. He said, "I know that God told me to preach this message." I might add that he very seldom made such statements or became noticeably frustrated when people did not respond to an altar call. I was standing and weeping, wondering if this was my time to be baptized in the Spirit. I closed my eyes as I looked up toward heaven. Then I had a vision. I saw a place that was pitch dark; suddenly, what looked like a door swung open allowing a piercing bright light to shine forth. Out of the bright light walked a person dressed in a robe. I could not clearly see anything except that he lifted his hands upward and forward as though he was praying. Jesus was praying for us. Jesus was praying for me. I immediately pushed out of my way a young man who was standing next to me in the pew, and I ran to the front of the church. That evening, I prayed for a long time. I was unaware of what was going on around me. After a long time I realized that most of the teens were praying for me as well as some adults. They were laying hands upon me, interceding for me to be baptized with the Holy Spirit. Praise be to God, the Father, for a group of people who could pray you through! That night I experienced my personal Pentecost, even though I only uttered a few groans. The pastor encouraged me to continue praying in the Spirit and assured me that my spiritual language would grow. He reminded me that this was just the beginning and not the end. God would show up in special times and continue to work in my life. I left church that night knowing that Jesus was alive and that he had done something very special in my life.

I began this essay with a testimony in order to emphasize the importance of a narrative-praxis approach to doing theology. Praxis, as a method, unites practice (doing) and theory (knowing) into the same reflective activity. A praxis approach encourages a critical engagement of theological reflection while affirming that our religious experiences shape our beliefs, and our beliefs shape our activities—hence theory and practice are inseparable and mutually informing.[3] By narrative, I mean

3. "Instead of theory leading to practice, theory becomes, or is seen in, the reflective moment in praxis." From this perspective, "theory arises from praxis to wield further

to highlight the importance of understanding Scripture as a grand meta-narrative with the Gospels and Acts as the heart of the Christian story. Jesus Christ is the center and leader of Christianity; therefore, a narrative theology will emphasize the priority of the story of Jesus Christ and its significance for the Christian community and for the world. This is not to suggest that narrative theology is not concerned with other doctrines, but it is to suggest that all doctrinal discussions in the end will come back to the theological center—Jesus Christ.[4] Therefore, narrative theology will pay close attention to the contours of the Christian story.

By sharing this testimony, I also wanted to draw attention to the importance of the worshipping community as the contextual arena for the discussion of theology including the sacraments (pneumatic ecclesiology).[5] Along with this is the importance of placing the sacraments within the theological framework of the way of salvation.[6] The Pentecostal *via salutis* is a dynamic pneumatic soteriology. The sacraments are significant symbolic signs that bring transformative grace by bringing people into closer contact with the saving action of Jesus. Therefore, the sacramental ordinances are community acts of worship for the individual-in-community and the community as a whole that provides necessary opportunities for spiritual nourishment on our communal journey in the Spirit.[7]

Ted Peters, a systematic theologian writes, "If we were to think of Christian systematic theology as a wheel, the Gospel of Jesus Christ would be located at the center. It is the hub around which everything else revolves . . . the gospel is that which establishes one's identity as Christian."[8]

---

praxis." Cheryl Bridges Johns, *Pentecostal Formation: Pedagogy among the Oppressed* (JPTSup, 2; Sheffield: Sheffield Academic, 1993) 37.

4. Gerard Loughlin, *Telling God's Story: Bible, Church and Narrative Theology* (Cambridge: Cambridge University Press, 1996) preface. See also his essay, "The Basis and Authority of Doctrine," in *The Cambridge Companion to Doctrine*, ed. Colin E. Gunton (Cambridge: Cambridge University Press, 1997) 41–64, esp. 52–54.

5. The Church is a relational *koinonia* that provides the proper context for the celebration of the sacraments among God's people. See Dwight W. Vogel, *Food for Pilgrims: A Journey with Saint Luke* (Akron, OH: OSL, 1996) 32.

6. John Christopher Thomas called for this in his presidential address to the Society for Pentecostal Studies. See his "Pentecostal Theology in the Twenty-First Century," *Pneuma* 20 (1998) 3–19. I am following and further developing his insightful suggestion to connect a biblical sign with each of the theological themes of the Fivefold Gospel.

7. Bernard Cooke, *Sacraments and Sacramentality* (Mystic, CT: Twenty-third, 1994) 6–11.

8. Ted Peters, *God—The World's Future* (Minneapolis: Fortress, 1992) 43–44.

Peters defines "gospel" as "the act of telling the story of Jesus with its significance." He further states that, "the gospel is the content of the story of Jesus and its significance; and this constitutes the material norm for systematic theology."[9] As a systematic theologian, Peters, like narrative theologians, recognizes the necessity of relating and integrating theological doctrines into the story of Jesus Christ. Therefore, any discussion of the sacraments must demonstrate a tight connection to the Gospel and the significance of the sacramental ordinance for the worshipping community.

Now you may be wondering what this has to do with the sacraments and a Pentecostal *via salutis*? The previous discussion of the centrality of the Gospel for narrative and systematic theology has *everything* to do with demonstrating the coherent and cohesive integration of sacraments into Pentecostal theology and the Pentecostal *via salutis*. Pentecostalism, from its very inception, has purposefully placed Jesus and the Full Gospel right at the center of its beliefs and practices.[10] Furthermore, I hope to demonstrate the need to re-vision the traditional Pentecostal understanding of ordinances into sacramental ordinances while simultaneously demonstrating that Pentecostal theology can be structured around the central narrative convictions of our story.[11]

For Pentecostals, the significance of the story of Jesus is articulated through the proclamation of the "Full Gospel" or "Fivefold Gospel": Jesus proclaimed as Savior, Sanctifier, Spirit Baptizer, Healer, and Coming King.[12] The Full Gospel functions as the central narrative convictions of the Pentecostal community. Pentecostal identity is articulated by the Full Gospel, which places Jesus at the center of God's dramatic redemptive story; and Pentecostals, as the end-time people, are participating in the latter rain. The community's proclamation of the Gospel is the primary

9. Ibid., 44.

10. See Donald Dayton, *Theological Roots of Pentecostalism* (Peabody, MA: Hendrickson, 1987). I am not suggesting that theological reflection is simply restating the Gospel. I believe all theological discourse is a secondary reflection on the primary source—the Scriptures, informed by experience, with the Gospel being the very heart of the Christian story.

11. See chapter 2 in this volume.

12. See Donald Dayton, "Introduction," in *Transforming Power: Dimensions of the Gospel*, ed. Yung Chul Han (Cleveland, TN: Pathway, 2001) 11–18. Dayton writes, "for a decade or so all of Pentecostalism was sharply Wesleyan/Holiness until this theme was suppressed by some under the influence of W. H. Durham" (13).

means of grace that channels the redemptive activity of God in Christ Jesus through the Holy Spirit to the community and into the world.

For Pentecostals, the Full Gospel needs to function overtly in our theological structure. The Full Gospel emphasizes the story of Jesus and its significance for the Pentecostal community. Ted Peters' analogy of the "hub" works well for a Pentecostal theology integrated into the Fivefold Gospel or Full Gospel. The theological center is the person Jesus Christ, and protruding out of the center are the five spokes which serve to explain the significance of the story of Jesus Christ. These spokes are the central narrative convictions of the Pentecostal story. They are theological themes, which are doxological in nature and bring coherence to the Pentecostal story and provide stability for the rest of Pentecostal theology. Our Pentecostal doctrinal practices and beliefs are the wheel, connected to and stabilized by the spokes while turning and spinning around its center—Jesus Christ. Pentecostal beliefs and practices, therefore, will always flow back to its center where it finds its ultimate significance. Jesus, then, is the primordial and ultimate sacrament.[13]

Even the so-called ordinances of the Pentecostal community must find their legitimization in Jesus.[14] In order for the Pentecostal community to embrace an act as an ordinance, there would need to be a firm belief that Jesus Christ had ordained it.[15] From this perspective the ordinances are understood to be "acts of commitment" practiced out of loyalty to Christ.[16]

---

13. See Herbert Vorgrimler, *Sacramental Theology*, trans. Linda M. Maloney (Collegeville, MN: Liturgical, 1992) 30–32.

14. In the U.S., Pentecostal denominations that are more influenced by the Wesleyan holiness tradition (like the COG) officially adhere to three ordinances (Water baptism, Footwashing and Communion) whereas those Pentecostal denominations more influenced by finished work holiness traditions, such as AOG, officially adhere to two ordinances (Water baptism and Communion). Although for other Pentecostal denominations and groups this may not necessarily be the case.

15. Pentecostals follow "Protestant orthodoxy" in that only "what can be traced back to an express ordinance of Christ and is bound up with his especial promise counts as a sacrament." Jürgen Moltmann, *The Church in the Power of the Spirit: A Contribution to Messianic Ecclesiology* (Minneapolis, MN: Fortress, 1993) 200.

16. See Sanely J. Grenz, *Theology for the Community of God* (Grand Rapids: Eerdmans, 2000) 514–18, who maintains the importance of retaining the word ordinance, but also argues that the ordinances are channels for the Holy Spirit to work in the lives of Christians, thus becoming more than memorial rites.

Unfortunately, for various reasons, some Pentecostals deny any real grace being mediated through the participatory ordinance to the community, thus reducing these mysteries to mere memorial rites, occasions solely for cognitive reflection devoid of the Spirit's presence and power.[17] Yet the expectation of the worshipping community is that they will encounter the presence of Christ through the Spirit in these celebrative activities.[18]

The concept of "ordinances" must be re-visioned because in Pentecostal worshipping communities these rites provide sacramental experiences for the faith-filled participants. In other words, baptism, footwashing and communion have "provided many with a context for experiencing the redemptive and sanctifying presence of God in great power."[19] These are redemptive experiences, for they provide worshippers with opportunities for the ongoing spiritual formation of being conformed to the image of Christ through encountering the Spirit of Christ through the participatory reenactment of the story of Jesus.

Pentecostal spirituality is conceived as a "way of life" that recognizes significant crisis experiences.[20] These experiences make possible the infusion of the dynamic presence of the Holy Spirit into our lives. Pentecostal

---

17. Frank Macchia, "Tongues as a Sign: Towards a Sacramental Understanding of Tongues," *Pneuma* 15 (1993) 61–76, writes, "most Pentecostals are uncomfortable with the term 'sacrament' because of association of the term with an 'institutionalization' of the Spirit with 'formalistic' liturgical traditions" (61). Unfortunately, his statement can be substantiated in the recent publication by William W. Menzies and Stanley M. Horton, *Bible Doctrines: A Pentecostal Perspective* (Springfield, MO: Logion, 1993). They write, "Biblical Christianity is not ritualistic or sacramental." The two ordinances ". . . are to be understood as occasions of memorial" (111). However, it must be pointed out that earlier Pentecostals may have been less troubled by the word "sacrament." For example, Aimee Semple McPherson calls communion and water baptism sacraments as well as ordinances.

18. See Frank D. Macchia, "Is Footwashing the Neglected Sacrament? A Theological Response to John Christopher Thomas," *Pneuma* 19 (1997) 239–49, esp. 241. On a personal note, I can recall various times of taking communion under the pastoral leadership of Richard Dobbins during the Annual Conference of the Ohio District Council of the Assemblies of God. We were encouraged to pray for God to bring physical and emotional healing as we participated in the communion meal. It was not merely a memorial meal; rather, we encountered the dynamic presence of Christ Jesus our healer because his body had been broken and bruised for our salvific healing.

19. Macchia, "Is Footwashing the Neglected Sacrament?" 240.

20. The *ordo salutis* is important to Pentecostals, but Pentecostalism must first and foremost be understood as a way of life.

soteriology that is more Wesleyan and thus more Eastern in orientation "emphasizes salvation as participation in the divine life more than the removal of guilt."[21] Salvation as "the Christian spiritual journey is a life lived in, through, and for God."[22] The sacramental ordinances, therefore, aid us in our salvific journey because they give the Holy Spirit necessary opportunities to keep the community on the right path—the way of salvation.

The sacramental ordinances become means of grace for the receptive individuals-in-community. The sacraments are not "magical actions" or simply "symbols of human response" but are effective means of grace when inspired by the Holy Spirit and received by genuine human response in faith.[23] The sacraments are prophetic narrative signs involving words and deeds through which the community can experience the redemptive living presence of God in Christ through the Holy Spirit.[24] The Spirit inspiring the act of commitment as the worshippers are responding in faith transforms it into effective sacramental experience.[25] The sacramental

---

21. Steven J. Land, *Pentecostal Spirituality: A Passion for the Kingdom* (Sheffield, UK: Sheffield Academic, 1993) 23.

22. M. Robert Mulholland Jr., *Shaped by the Word: The Power of Scripture in Spiritual Formation*, rev. ed. (Nashville: Upper Rooms, 2000) 26.

23. Clark H. Pinnock, *Flame of Love: A Theology of the Holy Spirit* (Downers Grove, IL: InterVarsity, 1996) 127, see also 123–29. I believe most Pentecostals would agree with Pinnock's statement, "the effectiveness of the sacraments is bound up with the Spirit and faith" (123). See also John Wesley's sermon "The Means of Grace," in *John Wesley's Sermons: An Anthology*, eds. Albert C. Outler and Richard P. Heitzenrater (Nashville: Abingdon, 1991) 158–71.

24. For the importance of the sacraments as prophetic, I am indebted to Daniel Tomberlin, a recent MDiv graduate at the Church of God Theological Seminary (now named Pentecostal Theological Seminary), who has served many years in the pastorate. He testified to how the Holy Spirit led him to have a footwashing service in which he washed the feet of an African-American pastor who was visiting his church. The church was located in the only city in Georgia that experienced race riots during the "Rodney King" riot. The event brought a deep conviction to some, thus taking on a prophetic nature.

25. Clark H. Pinnock in "Divine Relationality: A Pentecostal Contribution to the Doctrine of God," *Journal of Pentecostal Theology* 16 (2000) 3–26, articulates the importance of the relational dynamic in Pentecostal soteriology which is always initiated through God's grace but also requires human response. He writes, "Grace makes Spirit Baptism possible but people must seek the experience or it will not happen" (12). A Wesleyan Pentecostalism is much more "Eastern" in its understanding of the cooperation between the human and Divine, see Veli-Matti Kürkkäinen, *Pneumatology: The Holy Spirit in Ecumenical, International, and Contextual Perspective* (Grand Rapids: Baker Academic, 2002) 67–72, for a review of the "Eastern understanding" of the human and divine.

ordinances are metaphorical-narrative signs that re-enact the redemptive story of Jesus for the community. The community anticipates and participates in this redemptive activity through proleptic worship encounters with the living God.[26] During worship "time and space (are) fused and transcended in the Spirit" through proleptic foretastes of the coming promise and through the recapitulation of past biblical experiences. "Pentecostals (travel) in the Spirit forward or backward in time—back to Sinai, back to Calvary, back to Pentecost—forward to Armageddon, the Great White Throne judgment, the Marriage Supper of the Lamb."[27] In this manner, the sacraments "function socially if not ontologically to identify us as Christian"[28] by allowing the community to participate in the divine life. Furthermore, the sacraments provide sustaining nourishment for us during our journey and needful opportunities to reshape our identity as the eschatological messianic community.[29]

Based upon the previous discussion of Pentecostal worship, I have linked sacrament to ordinance. In doing so, I want to emphasize the role of the Holy Spirit in these mystical community acts of worship. Furthermore, in order for a rite to be constituted as a sacramental ordinance it must be directly linked to the Gospel and Jesus Christ. There are other sacraments and sacramental experiences, but I am concerned here to identify the sacramental ordinances because they are directly connected to the Gospel. From this perspective we could say that they are "Full Gospel" sacraments.

26. I am indebted to my colleague, R. Hollis Gause, for this important descriptive insight into the mystical character of Pentecostal worship. For more detailed discussion of Pentecostal worship as eschatological and sacramental see the theologically rich essay by Cheryl Bridges Johns, "What Makes a Good Sermon? A Pentecostal Perspective," *Journal for Preachers* 26 (2003) 45–54, esp. 46–49.

27. Land, *Pentecostal Spirituality*, 55. This "proleptic" dimension is not unique to Pentecostal worship, but I would suggest it is more than cognitive reflection. See Ted Peters, *God—the World's Future*, who makes "proleptic consciousness" an integral feature of his systematic theology (19).

28. Peters, *God—The World's Future*, 277.

29. See James F. White, *The Sacraments in Protestant Practice and Faith* (Nashville, TN: Abingdon, 1999). White's informative discussion of the Sacraments in the history of Protestantism focuses on four traditions (Methodist, Presbyterian, Episcopal and Lutheranism), yet his comments concerning Pentecostal worship reinforce my argument. White states that the real presence of Christ through the ministry of the Holy Spirit was a basic given of all Pentecostal worship, not just during communion (83). He further writes, "Modern-day Pentecostals often sound deeply eschatological with their worship heavily imbued with the present activity of the Holy Spirit. These gifts of the Spirit indicate the imminent return of Christ" (99).

Pentecostal Spirit baptismal testimonies make sense when they are understood within the *gestalt* of the Pentecostal Full Gospel message. As I have reflected on my own experience and the Spirit baptism testimonies of others, I am convinced not only that water baptism, footwashing, and the Lord's Supper are sacramental ordinances but also that Spirit baptism is a sacramental redemptive experience in which tongues serves as the prophetic sign.[30] If Spirit baptism is sacramental, as I believe Frank Macchia has demonstrated, then it too must be integrated into the Pentecostal *via salutis*[31] and be recognized as a sacramental ordinance of Pentecostal churches.

THE FULL GOSPEL AND ITS SACRAMENTAL ORDINANCES

Jürgen Moltmann, in *The Church in the Power of the Spirit*, poses an important question during his discussion of the sacraments.[32] Moltmann suggests, "churches with a plurality of sacraments must be asked about the

30. See Frank D. Macchia, "Tongues as a Sign: Towards a Sacramental Understanding of Pentecostal Experience," *Pneuma* 15 (1993) 61–76.

31. There is debate about this in both the finished work Pentecostal camp and the Wesleyan Pentecostal camp. For example, there are prominent scholars like William and Robert Menzies, Assemblies of God theologians, who see Spirit baptism as a vocational calling, thus falling strictly under ecclesiology and mission and not contributing to one's spiritual relationship with God ontologically, psychologically, or ethically. The fruit of the Spirit, the ethical-spiritual dimension of the Spirit, is received fully at conversion (based upon their reading of the Pauline corpus) yet the empowerment or Baptism of the Spirit comes subsequent to regeneration and is strictly for the purpose of mission (according to their interpretation of Luke-Acts). See William W. Menzies and Robert P. Menzies, *Spirit and Power: Foundations of Pentecostal Experience* (Grand Rapids: Zondervan, 2000) 189–208. However, there are also publications by AOG theologian Frank Macchia who argues persuasively that Spirit baptism should be understood as a sacramental sign, thus Spirit baptism contributes to one's salvific relationship with God; see his "Groans Too Deep for Words: Towards a Theology of Tongues as Initial Evidence" in *Asian Journal of Pentecostal Studies* 1.2 (1998) 149–73. Coming out of the Church of God (a Wesleyan Pentecostal denomination), see an earlier theological work by COG theologian Donald N. Bowdle, *Redemption Accomplished and Applied* (Cleveland, TN: Pathway, 1972). Bowdle writes, "the baptism with the Holy Spirit . . . important as it is, does not really find place within *ordo salutis*, since it pertains not to salvation but to service." Because it pertains to the power of the Church and not with soteriology, "the baptism with the Holy Spirit is properly concerned with ecclesiology" (61). However, for a Wesleyan Pentecostal view from a COG theologian, which affirms Spirit baptism as an essential part of the *ordo salutis* subsequent to regeneration and sanctification, see R. Hollis Gause, *Living in the Spirit: The Way of Salvation* (Cleveland, TN: CPT, 2009).

32. Jürgen Moltmann, *The Church in the Power of the Spirit: A Contribution to Messianic Ecclesiology* (Minneapolis: Fortress, 1993). For his discussion on the sacraments see chapter 5, "The Church in the Presence of the Holy Spirit," 197–288.

unified ground to which these sacraments are related, and why these acts in particular are called sacraments, and others are not."[33] In response to these important questions, I would argue with John Christopher Thomas that the unifying ground for the integration of the Pentecostal sacraments is the Fivefold Gospel.[34] The sacraments are directly connected to proclamation of the Gospel and specifically connected to commands and promises of Jesus Christ. In this light, Pentecostals who embrace the Fivefold Gospel might consider expanding the number of sacraments from three to five.[35] By connecting a sacramental ordinance with a significant sign to each of the theological doxological declarations concerning Jesus (Savior, Sanctifier, Spirit Baptizer, Healer, and Coming King), a coherent Pentecostal narrative theology would emerge from within the tradition and from the ground up.[36] Pentecostal theology would be a coherent and cohesive reflection of our relational experiential encounters with God in

---

33. Moltmann, *Church in the Power of the Spirit*, 199–200.

34. Thomas, "Pentecostal Theology in the Twenty-First Century," 19.

35. For Pentecostals who have dropped Jesus as Sanctifier from their Gospel message (mostly those in the finished work tradition), they should at least expand theirs to four by including Spirit baptism and Healing. However, some in the AOG tradition, like Simon Chan, are calling for a return to the more historic Fivefold message in order to reaffirm the importance of sanctification and to ensure a healthy integration between empowerment and holiness. See his *Pentecostal Theology and the Christian Spiritual Tradition* (Sheffield: Sheffield Academic, 2000) 69–70. By reasserting the importance of sanctification as a crisis experience(s), one is signaling a return to a more Wesleyan and Eastern soteriological paradigm. One could affirm sanctification from a Wesleyan perspective by re-visioning the traditional Wesleyan holiness view in terms of a more dynamic crisis-process dialectical understanding without giving up the importance of the consecrating moment(s). See, for example, James P. Bowers, "A Wesleyan-Pentecostal Approach to Christian Formation," *Journal of Pentecostal Theology* 6 (April 1995) 55–86. The retrieval of sanctification would only reinforce the importance of holiness in the Pentecostal life. All Pentecostals realize that holiness is not an option and that sanctification is a necessary aspect of being Christian. Those denominations that reject the traditional Wesleyan holiness notion of a second work of grace could still retain Jesus as Sanctifier and articulate a more dynamic soteriology that allows for sanctification to include both psychological and ontological dimensions.

36. Coherence refers to the integration of sacramental signs into the Fivefold Gospel, thus reinforcing the validity of the Pentecostal "truth claim" concerning our theological tradition. For an argument concerning Spirit baptism with tongues as a "coherent" truth claim see Amos Yong, "'Tongues of Fire' in the Pentecostal Imagination: the Truth of Glossolalia in Light of R. C. Neville's Theory of Religious Symbolism," *Journal of Pentecostal Theology* 12 (1998) 73–81.

Christ through the Holy Spirit—a distinctly Pentecostal theology from beginning to end.

A formal presentation of Pentecostal theology can discuss the various Christian doctrines but should do so in a manner which is in keeping with our own tradition.[37] This form of Pentecostal theology would be more *narrative* in its character and *systemic* in nature. In keeping with its spirituality, Pentecostal theology would begin with the importance of Jesus Christ and his story.[38] As Thomas suggests, the Fivefold Gospel should be the integrating paradigm of our theology.[39] The Fivefold Gospel articulates the central narrative convictions of the Pentecostal community that serves to explain *who* we are, *why* we exist, and *what* we are to do. In this manner, Pentecostal theology builds from the ground up because soteriology and ecclesiology are the primary, dynamic contexts of the manifestation of the social economic Trinitarian life. For the heart of our Pentecostal knowledge of God is the revelatory encounter with the living Christ that initiates us into an exciting redemptive covenantal journey with the Social Trinity.[40] All doctrinal discussions would find their ultimate significance and understanding in relationship to the "hub" (Jesus Christ) and its *spokes* (the Fivefold Gospel) contextualized within the worshipping Pentecostal community. In the remaining portion of this essay, I will briefly sketch out the connections between sacraments and Fivefold Gospel.[41]

Jesus is our Savior. He has ransomed us from the captivity of the kingdom of spiritual darkness and has reconciled us to God our Father. Jesus is our atoning sacrifice. Jesus is the pioneer and perfecter of our

37. Terry Cross, "The Rich Feast of Theology: Can Pentecostals Bring the Main Course or Only the Relish?" *Journal of Pentecostal Theology* 16 (2000) 27–47, esp. 33–34.

38. See Clark H. Pinnock, "Divine Relationality: A Pentecostal Contribution to the Doctrine of God," *Journal of Pentecostal Theology* 16 (2000) 3–26. Pinnock writes, "they [Pentecostals] do theology in the form of story and song. They should not develop theologies which are in tension with this feature" (11).

39. Thomas, "Pentecostal Theology in the Twenty-First Century," 17.

40. Cheryl Bridges Johns, "Healing and Deliverance: A Pentecostal Perspective," in *Pentecostal Movements as an Ecumenical Challenge*, eds. Jürgen Moltmann and Karl-Josef Kuschel, Concilim, 3 (Maryknoll, NY: Orbis, 1996) 47.

41. See Thomas, "Pentecostal Theology in the Twenty-First Century," 18–19. The following is a narrative-oriented elaboration and expansion of Thomas's insightful proposal to correlate a biblical sign with each "fold" in the Fivefold confession of Jesus, as follows: (1) Saviour—Water Baptism; (2) Sanctifier—Footwashing; (3) Spirit-Baptizer—Glossolalia; (4) Healer—Anointing with Oil; (5) Coming King—Lord's Supper.

faith (Heb 12:2). When a person calls upon the name of Jesus, repenting from sin and turning to God, they are saved. They experience justification and regeneration. They are born again and have the Holy Spirit. All future redemptive experiences spring forth from the seed sown in the initial experience of salvation.[42]

Water baptism is the sacramental ordinance that publicly proclaims one's new identity with Jesus and his community of followers. New converts are baptized with water because Jesus commanded us to do so (Matt 28:18–20). A believer's water baptism by immersion best reenacts the salvific experience of identifying with the death and resurrection of Jesus (Rom 6:4) for the forgiveness of sins (Acts 2:38). Water baptism recapitulates the protection of Noah and his family from divine judgment sent upon the wicked (Gen 6–9; 1 Pet 3:20–21) and also the Israelites' exodus deliverance through the waters of the Red Sea. Out of this, they emerged as a people belonging to God on the way to the Promised Land. Water baptism is the sacramental sign initiating one into the corporate *via salutis*.[43]

The focus of water baptism is on the candidate, yet the community not only witnesses the candidate's baptism but is also called by the Spirit to relive their initiating salvific experience, hence re-identifying themselves as part of the redemptive community—the body of Christ. It also serves to point us to the ultimate goal of salvation—glorification and the redemption of creation. It is a promise that creates hope and reshapes our identity as we proleptly participate in the redemptive experience. We are the eschatological community of God and, as this community, we function as a redemptive sacrament for the world—the body of Christ broken for the healing of the nations.

Jesus is our Sanctifier. He is our High Priest who intercedes for us praying that we would be sanctified (John 17). We realize that holiness flows from the very nature of the Holy Spirit through whom we partici-

---

42. This would include future redemptive experiences such as sanctification, healing, Spirit baptism and glorification. Thus there is a unitary interconnection of these identifiable and distinguishable experiences all anchored in the regeneration experience.

43. On Baptism, see Peters, *God—The World's Future*, 277–84; Grenz, *Theology for the Community of God*, 520–32; White, *Sacraments in Protestant Practice and Faith*, 31–72, 92.

pate in the divine life. Holiness is to permeate our entire being, affecting all aspects of our life as we continue in the *via salutis*.[44]

Footwashing serves as the sacramental activity by which we continue to experience God's redemptive cleansing and healing. The washing of one another's feet is a ceremony of cleansing. The sacrament reminds the community that as we travel this path we do get dirty through the contamination of the world, and, if we commit acts of sin, they can be forgiven. God has provided a means for forgiveness, purging and cleansing of sin along the *via salutis*.[45]

The sacrament recapitulates the biblical story of Israel's wanderings in the wilderness. It also involves recalling and reenacting Jesus's washing of the feet of the disciples (including Judas) prior to his crucifixion. As we wash each other's feet, we are reminded of our own shortcomings, yet we prolepticly experience God's declaration—your sins are forgiven. The community realizes it is a holy people and a royal priesthood. Communal holiness, wholeness, discipline, and discipleship are an integral aspect of traveling on the *via salutis*. Footwashing serves as a sacramental ordinance for continual need of spiritual cleansing during the journey to the promise land.

Jesus is our Spirit Baptizer. Jesus commanded his disciples to wait in Jerusalem for the gift of the Father (Luke 24:49; Acts 1:4). Peter proclaimed that this gift of the Father was for everyone who believed in Jesus Christ (Acts 2:38–39). John the Baptist testified that Jesus would baptize with the Holy Spirit (Mark 1:8).

The sacramental experience of Spirit baptism manifests in the personal, audible sign of *glossolalic* tongues that signifies the presence of the living God upon us and among us.[46] This sacramental experience is important for our empowerment as the charismatic missionary community. Signs and wonders follow those who preach the Gospel empowered by the Holy Spirit. Individuals-in-community are participatory witnesses to the redemptive acts of God for the world.

---

44. See R. Hollis Gause, "The Doctrine of Holiness," in *Transforming Power: Dimensions of the Gospel*, ed. Yung Chul Han (Cleveland, TN: Pathway, 2001) 87–147.

45. See John Christopher Thomas, *Footwashing in John 13 and the Johannine Community* (Sheffield, UK: Sheffield Academic, 1991) and Frank Macchia, "Is Footwashing the Neglected Sacrament?"

46. Frank Macchia, "Tongues as a Sign," 63, and also see his "Groans Too Deep for Words."

This sacramental experience, which breaks out into ecstatic moments of worship marked by ecstatic praise and compassionate weeping for the lost and hurting, draws one into a deep intimate relationship with the Holy Trinity. The sacrament of Spirit baptism empowers each believer to become an active and significant part of the charismatic missionary community. In this community, everyone is to be a priest and prophet ministering under the anointing of the Holy Spirit one to another and unto the world. The responsibility to reach the world with the transforming Gospel of Jesus Christ falls upon all in these last days, because the end is near.

Spirit baptism provides empowerment to be a witness of the Gospel, which flows out of relational intimacy with the Social Trinity. An intimacy forged in pilgrimage with the Spirit will be marked by periods of suffering and struggle, for the Spirit will lead one into the wilderness, as was Jesus, and into times of the "dark night of the soul." However, the presence and power of the living God does not leave us. The Spirit groans with us, even through us and causes us to weep and to shout as the Spirit of God comes down upon our community and as we proleptically glimpse the magnitude of our God and the glory of his Being.[47] The Word of God can become like "fire shut up in our bones" (Jer 20:9)—some may run, some may leap, and others may even weep. Spirit baptism is a mystical experience that is symbolized in *glossolalic* language, because it transcends the limits of human speech. Tongues are the expression of the mystical experience of union with and participation in God's triune being. Spirit baptism is a sacramental experience empowering the community to be a charismatic witness along the way to the city whose builder is God.

Jesus is our Healer. Jesus healed people of diseases and performed exorcisms, manifesting the presence of the Kingdom of God in a tangible restorative manner (Acts 10:38). Pentecostals confess that Jesus is "the same yesterday, today and forever" (Heb 13:10), and healing is an integral aspect of Jesus's ministry and atonement.[48]

The sacrament of healing involves the laying on of hands and anointing with oil (Mark 6:13 and Jas 5). Oil, along with the laying on of

---

47. Acts 2 recapitulates the Mount Sinai encounter as found in Exodus 19.

48. Menzies and Horton, *Bible Doctrines*, 189–207. See John Christopher Thomas, "The Devil, Disease and Deliverance: James 5.14–16," *Journal of Pentecostal Theology* 2 (1993) 25–50 and his *Devil, Disease and Deliverance: Origins of Illness in the New Testament* (Sheffield: Sheffield Academic, 1998).

hands, serves as the sacramental sign. "In the ministry of healing there is the expression of the belief that salvation and healing are for the whole person. The laying on of hands and anointing with oil are means whereby Pentecostals give expression to this belief."[49] Healing is not limited to just the physical but extends to the whole person; hence emotional or inner healing is also included.

The sacramental experience involves the community. When one is healed and testifies, it becomes a present proleptic sign of the future glorification that awaits all God's children. From this perspective, praying for the sick is an important aspect of Pentecostal communal worship because it allows God to break into the present. In turn, this allows the community to participate propleticly in the future promise of permanent healing (Revelation 19–20).

As we pray for those suffering, we are reminded that we live in the tension of the Kingdom of God—a kingdom present but not yet present. Those who are prayed for (even many times) and, yet, do not experience their healing are still recipients of God sustaining grace. Not everyone will be completely healed, yet all who participate in this sacramental act can experience sustaining grace through the abiding presence of the Spirit. The community is brought back to the reality that ultimate healing will take place in that great community experience of the second coming of Christ, when those who are both dead and alive, sick and healthy will be gathered up together in God. All healings are momentary testimonies of participating in the ongoing ministry of Christ through the power of the Spirit, and these same testimonial affirmations anticipate the coming of Christ.

Healing is an important sacramental ordinance that helps sustain us on this journey and shapes our identity as a compassionate, healing community. As a healing community, we welcome the poor, the lame, the weak, and the sick recognizing that their presence is a necessary sacrament for us. If they are not welcome, then the Spirit is not welcome. "The outcasts become vessels of honor through which God makes known the mysteries of His kingdom."[50]

Jesus is our Soon-Coming King. Jesus is coming soon to receive his eschatological community, his Bride. The sacrament of the Lord's Supper

---

49. Bridges Johns, "Healing and Deliverance," 49.

50. Ibid.

dramatically reenacts our Savior's death (1 Cor 11:23–26), but also pro-phetically recalls our Savior's promise that he will come again, and we, his people, will one day partake in that grand eschatological meal—the Marriage Supper of the Lamb (Matt 26:29).[51] At this meal we will dine in the fully-realized identity and dignity of being God's people, saved and sustained through the mission of the Son and Spirit!

The sacramental ordinance of the Lord's Supper, with its sign of the one cup and one loaf, gives us necessary opportunity for the Spirit to shape our identity as a collective people belonging to the one body of Christ. The superiority of one's race or gender is brought to prophetic condemnation; because, in Christ, we are one, servants one to another. If preference is given, it is to the weak, to the poor, to those suffering, for these are the ones whom Christ came to redeem (Luke 4:18–19). As we celebrate our liberation from satanic dominion and salvific union with God through Jesus's atoning life, ministry, death, and resurrection, we participate in the redemptive presence of the Almighty God who, through his Son and Spirit, has made a way for us. We are caught up in the divine dance in which we participate in the very being of God, longing for the fullness of his kingdom to be manifested. We partake in Jesus' body and blood to make us one and sustain us with his prophetic promise—"I am coming very soon." Maranatha!

The sacrament of the Lord's Supper allows us to partake in the body and blood of Christ. By it, we experience sustenance for our journey. It recapitulates the eating of *manna* in the wilderness as a means of sustaining the Israelites on their pilgrimage. The Lord's Supper is a sacramental event that shapes our identity as the messianic eschatological people of God. We look forward to Christ's coming, and we long and look forward to the coming of the Kingdom of God when God will be all and in all.

CONCLUSION

We are pilgrims on a journey—the *via salutis*. We were publicly initiated into this communal journey through water baptism. Along this journey the Lord has provided sanctifying cleansing through footwashing, spiritual empowerment through Spirit baptism, healing through anointing with oil, and spiritual sustenance through the bread and the wine—the body and blood of Jesus. These sacraments are means of grace providing

---

51.. See White, *Sacraments in Protestant Practice and Faith*, 73–118.

opportunities for the Spirit to work redemptively in the faithful participants within the Pentecostal proleptic worship service. The sacramental
ordinances evoke remembrance of the past and provoke playful anticipation of a future (promise) that collapses into the present mysterious
salvific experiences. This interplay between promise and fulfillment plays
a significant dialectical role creating opportunities of mystical redemptive
participation in the divine life of the community. I hope our understanding of ordinances takes on the mystical significance, which at the very
least transforms these particular 'acts of commitment' into *sacramental
ordinances*.[52]

JESUS ONLY IS OUR MESSAGE [53]

1. Jesus only is our Message,
Jesus all our theme shall be,
We will lift up Jesus ever,
Jesus only we will see.

(Chorus)
Jesus only, Jesus ever,
Jesus all in all we sing;
Savior, Sanctifier, Healer,
Baptizer and coming King.

2. Jesus only is our Savior,
All our guilt He bore away,
All our righteousness He gives us,
All our strength from day to day.

3. Jesus is our Sanctifier,
Cleansing us from self and sin,
And with all His Spirit's fullness,
Filling all our hearts within.

52. I agree with Robert L. Browning and Roy A. Reed, *The Sacraments in Religious Education and Liturgy: An Ecumenical Model* (Birmingham, AL: Religious Education, 1985), in their understanding of sacraments as means of grace whereby we communicate and participate in the good news of our faith. In this sense, sacrament is a translation of *mysterion*, thus a sacrament is not simply an ordinance of Christ (44).

53. *Gospel Hymns and Songs for Church Use* (Nigeria, West Africa: Zoe, n.d.) 44–45. This song attests to the centrality of the Fivefold Gospel. I am indebted to my colleague, Ayodeji Adewuya for sharing with me this hymn which testifies to the importance of our central narrative convictions.

4. Jesus only is our Healer,
All our sicknesses He bare,
And His risen life and fullness
All His members still may share.

5. Jesus only is our Power
His the gift of Pentecost,
Jesus, breathe Thy power upon us,
Fill us with the Holy Ghost.

6. And for Jesus we are waiting
Listening for the trumpet's sound,
Then it will be us and Jesus
Living ever with our God.

5

Pentecostal Prayer and Relational Openness
of the Triune God

God is not a metaphysical iceberg but a living person.

—Clark Pinnock[1]

*God has chosen to enter into a genuine relationship with his people,
and that relationship causes God himself to be vulnerable to abuse,
neglect, and personal injury. . . . Apparently, God's change of response shows that he is not mechanical in his response to sin and/or
repentance: rather his response is truly relational.*

—Lee Roy Martin[2]

T HE PURPOSE OF THIS essay is to present a Pentecostal "open theistic"
understanding (model) of God's knowledge.[3] I desire to reflect upon
the personal and relational aspects of the loving triune God's dynamic
interactive involvement with his children—a reflection centered in the

1. "Divine Relationally: A Pentecostal Contribution to the Doctrine of God," *Journal of Pentecostal Theology* 16 (April 2000) 3–26, 10.

2. "God at Risk: Divine Vulnerability in Judges 10:6–16," *Old Testament Essays* 18 (2005) 722–40, 735.

3. I prefer the term "Open theism" to "Freewill theism" even though they can be and, at times, are used interchangeably. Open theism draws more attention to the Social Trinity's ontological perichoretic reality of loving relationality. Freewill theism tends to place the emphasis upon humanity's ability to make choices; whereas, open theism points both to God's nature as an everlasting dynamic temporality and human libertarian freedom. Hence, the term open theism underscores God as entering into an authentic relationship with God's creation, especially humanity—a covenantal relationship that is vulnerable, that suffers, and is somewhat risky. See John Sanders, *The God Who Risks: A Theology of Divine Providence*, rev. ed. (Downers Grove, IL: InterVarsity, 2007) 197–220, esp. see chart on 218–19 for a succinct comparison of Classical theism, Freewill theism, and Open theism. He, too, prefers "openness" to freewill.

interesting
Concept.

Pentecostal community's worshipful practice of intercessory prayer.[4] Furthermore, I hope to show that an "Openness model" both reflects Pentecostal relational engagement with God and will continue to stimulate the Pentecostal community's further participatory proclamation of the Full Gospel in these "Last Days."

By the word "model" I mean a conscious and critical construction of my understanding of God rooted in my personal relationship with the living God (Social trinity). From this perspective, the model provides a sense of focus and meaningful understanding of one's relationship with God and creation. I do not want the model to "keep God in a box" nor should the model be confused with God. God is free to be God! I use the word model as a means to express my concept of God and God's relationship to his creation which in God reigns as loving sovereign Lord.[5] The model is informed by Scripture which is first and foremost understood as a grand narrative testifying truthfully of God and God's relationship with creation. The model is also informed by personal experience and interaction with a local Pentecostal community's experience of the Spirit.

As will be evident, the model that I will propose will be a modification of the traditional classical theistic model of God. The classical model of God is more akin to a "metaphysical iceberg" of the classical philosophers than the personal relational God presented in Scripture and passionately preached in our Pentecostal churches; namely, God is personal, holy, loving, suffering, dynamic and relational. This openness model is a critical reflection on Pentecostal spirituality and theological identity. The practices of personal and cooperate intercessory prayer and dynamic interactive worship services is the primary context and point of reference. I believe a warm kinship exists between the pietistic Wesleyan evangelical open theistic Christianity and Wesleyan-Arminian Pentecostal Christianity because we believe that our present prayers really impacts God, ontologically, and the future, potentially. A future that is not

4. As Clark H. Pinnock explains, "The model goes by other names than open theism. We choose this term because 'openness' was an attractive and unused metaphor which evoked the notion of God's open heart toward his creatures. It suggest a vision we have of God's glory which is characterized by voluntary (sic) self-limitation and self-sacrifice which extols divine power that delights more in nurturing than in subjugating creatures," 39, in his "Open Theism: 'What is this? A new teaching?—and with authority!' (Mk 1:27)," *Ashland Theological Journal* 34 (2002) 39–53.

5. I affirm that God created everything out of no preexistent matter and thus all things visible and invisible owe their existence to the creative activity of the social triune God.

yet entirely determined. We in cooperation with or even in resistance to God are writing the history of humanity; a story that has not yet been fully disclosed.

PRAYER: A TESTIMONY

During a Wednesday night worship service, a middle aged woman timidly walked up to the pastor and asked permission to share a testimony. After we finished praising God in song she was invited to come to the pulpit and share what the Lord had done in her life.[6] With tears trickling down her check she began to softly recall the traumatic crises that her family had been experiencing. Their 24-year-old son had been diagnosed with a rare cancer. The doctors at the Knoxville hospital recommended he be transferred to a hospital in Florida which specialized in treating the rare cancer. They traveled to Florida and went through a battery of tests again only to receive the same diagnosis. The doctors in Florida referred them back to Knoxville hospital because they could not treat his cancer any differently. They all agreed that it would be best for him to be close to his home and family as he went through the chemotherapy treatment. Those of us listening were drawn into her testimony and experienced momentarily some of the pain this family must have been going through. We knew her testimony must have a hope-filled ending since it was a healing testimony. We knew that somehow God had shown up in a miraculous way and changed the future for this family. But this knowledge did not keep me from quietly crying as I listened to my sister's testimony.

Her son had undergone the treatments, but later tests showed he still had some cancerous tumors. In fact, his situation was only getting worse. If doctors could not get the cancer to go into remission he would die. Once again, the doctors in Knoxville sent him back to the doctors in Florida in a final attempt to cure him. The day before surgery, after a series of test, they were amazed to discover that he was cancer free. A loud shout went up before the Lord Jesus, our healer, in the sanctuary that night as we celebrated with her. We gave thanks to God for the gracious miracle. She thanked the church folk for praying with her during this great ordeal.

6. The following is my recollection of an oral testimony that was shared with the congregation at Woodward Church of God, Athens, Tennessee on November 28, 2001. Woodward is a classical Pentecostal Church with a strong emphasis upon the Fivefold Gospel, laity involvement, and experiential celebrative worship services which generally culminate in "altar calls."

Her son's life had been spared through the miraculous touch of the living God. She was convinced that God healed her son because people were praying.

yes .   Pentecostals believe that corporate and personal prayer can change things; it impacts God and God in turn responds. Hence, God is a living, dynamic, personal being who can presently intervene and change situations dramatically. God touches lives, changes character and sometimes alters situations in such a way that God is proclaimed by His people, just as in biblical times, to have wrought a miracle. Therefore, Pentecostals are not "cessationists."[7] They believe that the living God still acts as miraculously today as in the past.

I began this theological inquiry with a testimony because I believe we must anchor our theological reflection into a worshipping community. Hence this discussion finds its immediate context within a Pentecostal worshipping community—a community that regularly practices intercessory prayer.

I am not saying Pentecostals, including myself, always pray properly, pray with right motives, pray from sound theological perspectives, or even that prayer determines God's ongoing creative activity. What I am saying is that our way of praying should be allowed to shape our way of believing. Prayer is not something we do after we have our theology in place—prayer is doing theology.

Our way of praying indicates that we, because of God's grace, can enter into a dynamic reciprocating relationship of rich fellowship with the Social Trinity. God encourages us to participate with him in creating the future.[8] This understanding of dialogical prayer which anticipates God to respond according to his promises challenges some of the basic assumptions of classical theism.[9]

---

7. See Jon Ruthven, *On the Cessation of the Charismata: The Protestant Polemic on Post Biblical Miracles* (Sheffield, UK: Sheffield Academic Press, 1993).

8. See John Sanders, *The God Who Risks: A Theology of Providence* (Downers Grove, IL: InterVarsity, 1998) 271–75.

9. Henry H. Knight III in *A Future for Truth: Evangelical Theology in a Postmodern World* (Nashville: Abington, 1997) 165, summarizes the classical theistic model as "the detached, immutable, timeless, omnipotent, omniscient and impassible deity whose attributes are defined more by Greek philosophy than biblical revelation." See chapter 8 for Knight's critiques on the classical notion of impassibility and eternity. For a critique of open theism and contemporary restatement of a classical theistic view of God see Norman Geisler, *Creating God in the Image of Man?: The New "Open" View of God-*

PRAYER: A HOMILY

Before moving on, I will make a few comments on one familiar biblical passage. This will anchor my discussion into the biblical witness of God's revelation to humanity. The passage, Exodus 32, narrates Moses's intercessory prayer campaign on behalf of the "stiff-necked," wayward Israelites. In this passage, we are told that God becomes very angry at the Israelites because they are committing idolatry. God tells Moses that He is going to wipe out the Israelites and make Moses into a great nation (Exod 32:1–10). Moses intercedes for the people (Exod 32:11–14). Moses says to the living God, "Turn from your fierce wrath; change your mind and do not bring disaster on your people. Remember Abraham, Isaac and Jacob ..." (Exod 32:12–13, NRSV). Moses challenges God to be patient and persistent with the people and not to forget his promise made to Abraham, Isaac, and Jacob. As a result of Moses's conversation with God, we are told, "the Lord changed his mind about the disaster that he planned to bring on his own people" (Exod 32:14 NRSV). Moses's prayerful dialogue with God had an impact on God so that God *changed* his mind about what he *had planned* to do!

This biblical narrative presents us with a passionate God who can be affected by people. God is a real person who has passions and feelings like mercy, compassion, love, and anger. In Exodus 32, God is described as becoming hot with anger. We are told that he was planning to wipe out his people because of his justifiable anger. Yet, Moses's dialogical intervention diverts God's justifiable wrath. "God takes Moses' contribution with upmost seriousness." Moses was able to change God's mind because "God treats the conversation with Moses with integrity and honors the human insight as an important ingredient for the shaping of the future."[10]

John Goldingay's comments about this passage are insightful. He writes, "If we want to be philosophical (in a certain sort of way), of course, we can say that God knew ahead of time that the moment would come for a change of mind and that was all part of the plan. We may prefer to safeguard God's sovereignty in this way. But the Bible does not do so." Biblical narrative, like this passage, portrays God's response to Moses as a real response. We are not told in brackets, "Now, of course, God knew

---

Neotheism's Dangerous Drift (Minneapolis, Minnesota: Bethany, 1997).

10. Terence E. Fretheim, *The Suffering of God: An Old Testament Perspective* (Philadelphia: Fortress, 1984) 50–51.

ahead of time that Moses would pray that way, and God had made allowance for that." If this had been so would God's response really have been a response?"[11] The Calvinistic perspective suggests God predetermined the event before creation. The Arminian perspective suggests that God simply foreknew everything before it came to pass. If God already knew what was already going to transpire, would that really be an authentic response on God's part? Would that really have been a response at all?

Exodus 32 is not saying God foreknew or that God had predetermined; it is saying that God, in the experiential reality of time-space, made up his mind that he was going to wipe out Israel and, then, decided not to. Wow! What kind of God is this that he would create people in his own image and invite them to participate in some of his decision-making? This, of course, requires God to suspend some of his ability to know the future. This is not the God of the philosophers who creates a *perfect* being according to their understanding and then make biblical passages fit into it. No, "God is not an abstract entity up there on top of the mountain or an impassive monarch sitting on a throne in heaven. God is not an idea or merely the ground of my being."[12] God cannot be known through abstract analytical deductive reasoning, or philosophic syllogisms. He can be known only through fellowshipping with Him. Scripture, especially biblical narrative, presents us the living God, who is a passionate person. God is vulnerable to his creation by limiting himself so that he can enter into an authentic covenant relationship with those who respond to his grace. God beckons his people to personally participate in his creation. "God invites us into the fulfillment of the divine purpose for the world. Thus, when we pray, things happen (or are prevented from happening)."[13]

As a Pentecostal, I firmly believe that prayer changes things. Prayer is a primary means to moving the hand of God. God does indeed respond to his children's prayers. As the above passage of Scripture and testimony indicated, we recognize that God does respond to peoples' prayers in ways that change the future prognosis of individuals and even nations. The young man would have died if God had not intervened. His mother and our church believe God healed the young man in response to prayer. Our Pentecostal ways of praying (which I would argue

11. John Goldingay, *Walk On: Life, Loss, Trust and Other Realities* (Grand Rapids: Baker Academic, 2002) 41–47, 46.

12. Ibid., 42.

13. Ibid., 46.

is modeled after the prayers of biblical characters and Psalms of lament) challenges the Classical theistic concepts related to God's impassibility, eternality and omniscience. For the purpose of this essay, I will be primarily discussing one attribute, God's omniscience and the corollary concern of human free will.[14]

OMNISCIENCE AND HUMAN FREEDOM:
IDENTIFYING THE PROBLEM

Traditional Classical theism understands omniscience as God knowing absolutely and in complete totality all of reality—past, present and future. God knows everything, even the future, because God exists in the ever-present state of the eternal now which transcends space and time. God is every*where* and every-*when*. According to Classical theism, the triune God gazes upon all of reality simultaneously from the static position of the eternal now. The past, future and present are fixed and/or determined from God's point of view. However, we humans exist in a space-time continuum. We experience the passing of time, but these features of our creaturely existence do not apply to God.

If God knows the future, in an absolute sense, then God knows every event that had and will ever transpire. His creation—including humans—will act according to what God knows. If the Classical theistic model is true, how then can humans be authentically free to act? For example, if God knows that I will eat eggs for breakfast tomorrow then I will eat eggs even though I pondered the various limited options that were available to me (such as eggs, cereal or Slim-fast). Why did I choose *eggs*? Was it because I had real options? If God knew that I would choose eggs, then I eat eggs for breakfast. Furthermore, from God's position of the eternal now all of created reality had already begun and ended, thus what will happen from our perspective has already transpired from God's perspective.

Therefore, even though I intuitively experience a strong sensation that I had a real choice between eggs and cereal for breakfast, I really had no choice at all. Either God already simply knew I would eat eggs (Arminian foreknowledge) or God had predetermined what I, we, all of reality would do prior to creation (Augustinian-Calvinistic theological

14. All Christian traditions practice intercessory prayer, but how they understand the effects of such prayer may differ. Those traditions which embrace a biblical synergistic soteriology would most likely share a similar understanding of prayer.

determinism). Philosophical theologian Thomas Morris helps us to better appreciate this problematic issue:

> If God's knowledge is absolutely complete and he cannot possibly hold a false belief about anything, an argument can be constructed which seems to show that there cannot be any genuine freedom, any authentically free will, in the world at all.[15]

I agree with the Open theists that early Christian theologians were much too dependent upon Greek philosophical concepts in constructing their model of God; which is now identified as Classical theism.[16] We must, however, come to grips with the truth that we all draw upon philosophical concepts in constructing our worldviews which enable us to construct a working model of God. Pentecostals will want the Holy Spirit to inspire the Scripture in such a way that it becomes the primary material in constructing our understanding of the living God. If this were the case then why not turn to Scripture and solve the dilemma?

The Bible seems to support the classical theistic understanding of God's omniscience. God's knowledge appears to be presented as an absolute knowledge of past, present, and future events. At the same time, the Scripture also affirms human freedom as being self-determining. In places, the Bible seems to forcefully present God as deterministic. That is, not only does God know the future exhaustively, but God knows the future because God is the determinate cause. Yet, it is the same Bible which holds humanity as morally responsible agents of their actions. The tension seems to stand in the Bible without any attempt of a resolution.[17]

For example, the *texus classicus* of this biblical paradox is found in Acts 2:23. The context is that of the Apostle Peter's first sermon after Pentecost in which he explains the event and then calls people to repentance. Peter proclaimed that Jesus "was handed over to you by God's set purpose and foreknowledge; and you, with the help of wicked men, put him to death by nailing him to the cross" (NIV). The passage expresses both divine foreknowledge and human freedom. Thus, Scripture alone

---

15. Thomas V. Morris, *Our Idea of God: An Introduction to Philosophical Theology* (Downers Grove, IL: InterVarsity, 1991) 89.

16. See Clark Pinnock et al., *The Openness of God: A Biblical Challenge to the Traditional Understanding of God* (Downers Grove, IL: InterVarsity, 1994) 8–9.

17. See David Basinger and Randall Basinger, eds., *Predestination and Free Will: Four Views of Divine Sovereignty and Human Freedom* (Downers Grove, IL: InterVarsity, 1986).

generally does not resolve all theological differences. Scripture presents
the narrative of God which provides clear boundaries of what is and is not
acceptable beliefs and practices. The Bible is not a systematic textbook.
The Bible presents itself to Christian readers as an overarching theological story with the Triune God being the main character. Thus particular
verses of Scripture must be understood within the grand story. Scripture
alone does not resolve all theological conundrums. We must also look to
the Holy Spirit and community experience as necessary means to bring
resolution to some theological issues.

Theology is never simply a restatement of Scripture, even though
Scripture is theological narrative. The ongoing formation and articulation
of theology always involves community discernment of the Spirit, experience, and reason. Why not, then, allow our practice of worship and prayer
inform our theological model?[18] It is my conviction that a Pentecostal
worshipful engagement with the Social Trinity and faithful witness to the
world is more accurately presented by an "Openness" model. Furthermore,
an Openness model best reconciles this biblical antinomy concerning
divine foreknowledge and human freedom.[19] An Openness model further clarifies our Pentecostal concepts about the triune God as a social
dynamic being and the future.

AN "OPENNESS" MODEL: THE PENTECOSTAL OPTION

In the remainder of this chapter I will interact with two of the more traditional Christian theistic models of God in order to provide a backdrop

18. For an argument, that is a reversal of my concern to start with prayer rooted in
our salvation experience see Terrance Tiessen, *Providence and Prayer: How Does God
Work in the World?* (Downers Grove, IL: InterVarsity, 2000). He states that "We *should*
define our understanding of concerning the nature of God's action in the world and pray
accordingly," 15. Tiessen examines 11 models of providence and after each model he
offers a case study on prayer which is coherent with the theological model presented.

19. In reconciling the biblical paradox concerning divine omniscience and human
freedom, we must provide an adequate theodicy. William Hasker has highlighted the
issue of theodicy. He writes, "It is becoming increasingly clear that a satisfying response
to this problem requires some sort of positive account of God's reason for permitting the
evils which exist in the world." William Hasker, "Providence and Evil: Three Theories,"
Religious Studies 21 (1992) 91–105, 92. See further his latest work, *The Triumph of God
over Evil: Theodicy for a World of Suffering* (Downers Grove, IL: InterVarsity, 2008.
According to Hasker, "broadly stated, the philosophical problem of evil is the problem of
accounting for the evil in the world in light of a theistic conception of God, where God is
said to be prefect in knowledge, power and goodness," 16.

for an Openness model. I will present the model, and then evaluate it by the following criteria: Is the model faithful to the biblical narrative; does it hold together logically; does it offer a satisfying theodicy; and most importantly, does it reflect and reinforce the Pentecostal practice of prayer? Then I will sketch a Pentecostal Openness model and address some of the more problematic concerns associated with it. The two traditional models are Augustinian-Calvinistic Determinism and Arminian-Molinism. These two serve as overarching categories, but I feel they capture the basic and central concepts of various positions. The Open theistic model will be addressed last. By presenting alternative views I hope to further reinforce the need for Pentecostal theologians and ministers to rethink their theological model (which I suspect will probably be closer to the Arminian-Wesleyan position) and be more open to the Open theism position. I believe an Openness model more accurately reflects the Pentecostal community's worship and prayer practices, as well as the Pentecostal mission of reaching the world with the Full Gospel message.

AUGUSTINIAN-CALVINISTIC DETERMINISM

Augustinian-Calvinistic determinism takes in all views that present a deterministic account of human activity. This category emphasizes God's knowledge as being the cause of everything and God's sovereign ability to carry out his will. This understanding of God's sovereign control includes theologians like Augustine, Luther, Calvin, John Feinberg, R. C. Sproul, Norman Geisler, and Millard Erickson. The unifying characteristic of this group is that God knows the future exhaustively because he planned it down to the minutest detail prior to creating. Nothing could "be" other than it is, because God predetermined everything that would transpire. God's will is sovereign and immutable. In this model, God did not foresee the future free choices of his creatures. God predetermined everything in order to achieve his desired plan.[20] Feinberg reflects this strand of theological determinism. He writes, "God is absolutely sovereign, and thus possesses absolute self-determination. This means God's will covers

---

20. I am aware that there are variant positions, but they all are classical theists and would all adhere to some form of theological determinism whether hard or soft and generally argue that human freedom is compatible with determinism. See Paul Helm, "The Augustinian-Calvinist View" in *Divine Foreknowledge: Four Views*, eds. James K. Beilby and Paul R. Eddy (Downers Grove, IL: InterVarsity, 2001) 162–89.

all things, and the basis for God's sovereign choices is neither what God foresees will happen nor anything else external to his will."[21]

In fairness we must acknowledge that Feinberg does not represent all who embrace theological determinism.[22] But his statement does underscore the sovereignty, majesty, and glory of God which are central characteristics of this traditional model. Richard Rice's comments expound upon these characteristics and provide a helpful summary of the Augustinian-Calvinistic position.

> God's will is the final explanation for all that happens; God's glory is the ultimate purpose that all creation serves. In his infinite power, God brought the world into existence in order to fulfill his purposes and display his glory. Since his sovereign will is irresistible, whatever he dictates comes to pass and every event plays its role in his grand design. Nothing can thwart or hinder the accomplishment of his purpose. *God's relation to the world is thus one of mastery and control* (emphasis added).

The deterministic tradition draws upon Scripture to support its claims. The biblical descriptions of divine power, knowledge, and glory are too numerous to mention. For example, Isa 46:9–11 reads:

> I am God, and there is no other; I am God and there is none like me. I make known the end from the beginning from ancient times, what is still to come, I say: My purpose will stand and I will do all that I please. From the east I summon a bird of prey; from a far-off land, a man to fulfill my purpose. What I have said, that will I bring about; what I have planned I will do." (NIV)

If you follow this passage with Num 23:19: "God is not a man, that he should lie, nor a son of man, that he should change his mind. Does he speak and then not act? Does he promise and not fulfill?" And, follow it up with Mal 3:16: "I the LORD do not change," the argument appears to have been further fortified with emphatic biblical support. The Augustinian-Calvinistic explanations of passages like these with its emphasis on divine knowledge and sovereignty have exerted great influence upon Christianity.

Determinism, both philosophical and theological, is logically consistent. Since God had already decreed what would happen before creation.

21. See John Feinberg, "God Ordains All Things" in Basinger and Basinger, eds., *Predestination and Free Will*, 19–43, 29.

22. Besides Helm's essay mentioned above, see Norman Geisler's position "God Knows All Things" in Basinger and Basinger, eds., *Predestination and Free Will*, 61–84.

Because God is omnipotent, he will bring about all that he had predetermined. Thus, "theological" determinism is a correct label to apply to this tradition. However, in order to have a strong affirmation for Augustinian-Calvinistic concepts (predestation and individual election), we must silence certain portions of Scripture which express such notions as God's desiring to save all people; warnings about falling away from God; God changing God's mind; God being grieved; and the general implication that biblical characters influence God's future discussions and actions through their prayers.[23]

All forms of theological Determinism will inevitably weaken the notion of human free choice in order to maintain its interpretive justification of God's sovereignty, majesty and glory. Rice concisely points out the harsh logical consequences of this model:

> God's omnicausality involves omniresponsibility. If everything happens just the way he plans it, then God is responsible for everything. This excludes creaturely freedom, and it seems to make God responsible for all the evil in the world.[24]

Pinnock's comment is more succinct and speaks for all Open theists concerning the logical and biblical shortcomings of theological determinism. "Complete divine omniscience of all future states would rule out genuine freedom."[25] If God has exhaustive, definite foreknowledge, then it would make God the *direct* culprit of evil. It cannot overcome the logical consequence of its position. God is the Deterministic cause of everything; hence, humanity is not genuinely free, thus God is solely and directly responsible for evil.

In fairness, the Deterministic model does attempt to free God of moral guilt for angelic and human sin, but it does make God morally responsible for evil. This seems very difficult to reconcile with Scripture's view that God is holy-love and so relentlessly opposed to moral evil.[26] There are a variety of Deterministic models, which attempt to resolve

23 See Gregory A. Boyd, *The God of the Possible: A Biblical Introduction to the Open view of God* (Grand Rapids: Baker, 2000), a very readable presentation of Open theism that addresses the various biblical passages, showing how they can also be interpreted to support an Open theistic model.

24. "Divine Foreknowledge and Free-Will Theism" in *The Grace of God and the Will of Man*, ed. Clark Pinnock (Minneapolis: Bethany, 1989) 121–39, esp. 132.

25. Basinger and Basinger, *Predestination and Free Will*, 57.

26. William Hasker, "Providence and Evil: Three Theories," *Religious Studies* 21 (1992) 91–105, 94.

this problem. However, all of them collapse into a Deterministic fatalism which taints God's character by making God the sufficient cause, thus the culprit for all moral evil.

Some find the Deterministic model reassuring. Pastorally, the advantage of the Deterministic model is that it grants a high standard of security in the midst of difficulty for the believer. God is in absolute control.[27] Nothing is left to human choice or chance.

But would one want to sacrifice the biblical presentation of God's relational freedom to respond to humanity, especially intercessory prayer? What about the genuine experience of making choices—human freedom.[28]

By genuine human freedom, I mean that causal influences do not determine my every choice or action; however, they may influence my choices and/or actions in significant ways. A free choice, then, is an event in which "alternatives are noted, considered, evaluated in terms of some kind of criteria, and finally decide one way or the other."[29] This is not a radical freedom but is a libertarian view. Libertarian freedom maintains that I (we) could have acted differently then I (we) did. The choice was truly my decision. One theologian states it this way: the individual "was not compelled by causes either internal to himself (genetic structure or irresistible drives) or external (other persons, including God) to act as he did."[30] Even though there were causal influences, the person chooses to act in a *certain* way instead of a *different* way.

Another more serious shortcoming of the Deterministic model is that it cannot support a personal and interactive relationship between the triune God and humans. "True dialogue requires two independent participants, neither of which wholly controls the responses of the other."[31] In any version of the Deterministic model, this understanding of recip-

27 For example, see Eugene TeSelle, *Augustine* (Nashville: Abingdon, 2006) 38.

28. Furthermore, the model supports current society status quo and can lead to a passive fatalism. Things are the way they are because God predetermined it. How often has this argument been used to justify incompetent leadership and right to entitlement?

29. William Hasker, *Metaphysics: Constructing a World View* (Downers Grove, IL: InterVarsity, 1983) 44.

30. Bruce Reichenbach, "God Limits His Power" in Basinger and Basinger, *Predestination and Free Will*, 100–124, esp. 103.

31. William Hasker, "Providence and Evil: Three Theories," *Religious Studies* 21 (1992) 91–105, esp. 94.

rocating dialogue is lacking. Furthermore, how can one have a personal relationship with a God who is absolutely changeless? This view lacks the dynamic and dialogical relationship between God and creation, especially humanity (a central theme of Scripture). As a Pentecostal, I believe prayer changes things and influences God's actions. This is not because God determined how God would act prior to creation. God deliberates within space-time in the present through the Holy Spirit and in accordance with God's past promises. The limited yet multiple present activities of creation, and especially humanity in the present create potential realities for the future. The future changes as those potentialities become realities. The future is partially determined according to God's promises and yet partially open because of God's relational character to open up and enter into authentic relationship with and for creation. For me, the Deterministic model is unsatisfactory for any Pentecostal theology.

ARMINIAN-MOLINISM

Another compatibilistic argument is found within the Arminian—Molinism traditions. I recognize that these are two different traditions which are historically independent of each other.[32] However, both models assert: 1) God is essentially omniscient; 2) Human beings have a libertarian free will. Therefore I have included them within the same category. I will first examine the Arminian model then move to the Molinian model which is also called middle knowledge.

The Arminian model places great stress upon genuine human freedom while still adhering to the concept of absolute foreknowledge from a classical theistic perspective. God's knowledge is exhaustive. God knows the past, present, and future in complete detail. Arminians argue that God knows everything that will transpire, but God does not sufficiently cause it. God "simply" foresees the future free choices of his creatures thus knowing what will come to pass.[33]

32. For a clear presentation of Arminianism see David Hunt, "The Simple-Foreknowledge View" and for Molinism, see William Lane Graig, "The Middle-Knowledge View." Both essays are found in *Divine Foreknowledge*, eds. James K. Beilby and Paul R. Eddy (Downers Grove, IL: InterVarsity, 2001).

33. David Hunt, "The Simple-Foreknowledge View" in Beilby and Eddy, eds., *Divine Foreknowledge*, 67. Hunt is not sure how God knows the future but he convinced that "God simply *knows the future*."

This strong affirmation of creaturely freedom does help relieve God of being morally responsible for evil. "Evil originated in the misuse of creaturely freedom. It is not attributable to a defect in God's original design of the world."[34] God is indirectly responsible since God created humanity with a free will; however he is not directly causatively responsible. This model can demonstrate that absolute foreknowledge is not necessarily causative but only logically related to human choices. From my perspective the Arminian model is better situated to Pentecostal spirituality then the Deterministic model. Arminianism affirms a biblical synergistic understanding of soteriology, seems to offer a more satisfactory theodicy, and continues to affirm the biblical paradox.

However, the problem is that even though Arminians claim an interactive dynamic relationship exists between God and humans, there really is not one. As Rice notes: "The concept of absolute foreknowledge . . . the idea that God sees the entire future in advance is incompatible with the concept that God interacts with his creatures on a momentary basis."[35]

If God knows everything that will happen, it must come to pass or else he falsely believed something to be true that was not (which is logically impossible). Therefore, the future is fixed and the actual occurrence of the present and future contributes nothing to God's experience. God already enjoys whatever value the present and future reality may have along with that of his reaction to it.

Arminian models insist that human beings have the capacity for genuine free choice and self-determination. They also argue that God's knowledge and His will are responsive to creaturely action, thus divine foreknowledge is only logically related to future choices, not causatively related to them (God knew I would eat cereal, he did not necessarily cause me to eat cereal for breakfast). However, this model seems to logically collapse back into the static universe of the eternal now. God cannot freely act moment by moment because he has already known (by foreknowledge) how he will act. Human freedom is really an illusion because God already knows how they will act and how he will respond. Thus, it is logically impossible to do (x) after (t) if God knows before (t) that (x) will occur. Their argument may be that "my act is responsible for God's

---

34. Richard Rice, "Divine Foreknowledge and Free-Will Theism," in *The Grace of God and the Will of Man*, ed. Clark Pinnock (Minneapolis: Bethany, 1989) 133.

35. Richard Rice, "Divine Foreknowledge and Free-Will Theism," in Pinnock, ed., *The Grace of God and the Will of Man*, 133.

previous knowledge of it because God would have not foreknown it if I had not done it."[36] However, the problem remains; the future is known exhaustively and, thus, fixed.

The following analogy will help clarify my concern. I can go down to the local video center and rent a movie. This movie has already been filmed, thus the whole outcome is fixed. As I watch the movie, I can experience surprise, suspense, and even identify with a character's struggle to make a choice, but I have no ability to change the outcome of the movie. In fact, I can change nothing about the movie. In an Arminian model, creation including all free agents is acting out a very detailed screen play. God completely knows the story, even though the screen play has been written by the free choices of humans. There are no retakes, no edits, and no human improvisation. The present rolls into the future according to the already known knowledge of what has already happened. The point is that our present experience of reality is a "rerun" for God. God saw the whole movie once. The first viewing must have taken place at a certain time (prior to creation) or from a certain place (the eternal now). God is not the immediate cause of everything, but he does know it in its entirety because he saw it.

An Arminian model cannot escape the logical conclusion. For God, the movie is over; all that is left is for creation to play out the details. For us, we live in a fixed and static universe. Humanity does not experience it as such, but God most certainly does. If the future is foreknown, then genuine human freedom of the present becomes an illusion.[37]

In order to resolve the issue between God's knowledge and human agency, some theistic philosophers are presenting a Molinian model (middle knowledge). The middle knowledge model has become quite popular among contemporary Evangelicals who want to maintain both a traditional understanding of God's omniscience and genuine human free will.[38]

Middle knowledge attempts to demonstrate that God can know the future of free agents without causing their choice. Robert Cook, an advocate of this model, argues that God is aware of all future choices and

---

36. Linda Zagzebski, "Divine Foreknowledge and Human Free Will," *Religious Studies* 21(1985) 279–98, 290.

37. For further critique, see Kenneth J. Archer, "Open View Response to the Arminian View," *Pneuma Review* 7 (Winter 2004) 60–64.

38. [AQ ?]

hypothetical circumstances involving free, and therefore, unpredictable beings. The infinite array of hypothetical circumstances is sometimes referred to as "subjunctive conditionals of freedom" or "counterfactuals of freedom." A counterfactual of freedom is a proposition specifying how a free being would freely act if placed in a certain set of circumstances. "If placed in total circumstances C, person P would freely perform action A." In this manner, the middle knowledge model explains *how* God can know the future free choices of humans.

Like the Deterministic model it is logically consistent. It especially works well in a classical theistic model that articulates a "prefect being" theology. The concept of God as a perfect being, however, is shaped more by classical Greek philosophical categories and syllogistic argumentation, then by plain reading of Scripture.[39]

Middle knowledge does not support a satisfactory view of theodicy. Nor does it fully appreciate, as Pentecostals do, the dynamic personal relationship between the social triune God and humans. It cannot because God chooses which possible reality to bring into definite existence. Cook's statement reveals this: "God's sovereignty is to be understood in terms of his free choice as to which possible universe to actualize. Yet human freedom partially dictates the activities which each possible world contains."[40] Cook does not explain how human freedom partially dictates God's choice to actualize a possible world. Therefore, middle knowledge does not resolve the problem. The model explains "how" God can know the future, based upon counterfactuals of human freedom, but is not sure "how" humans participate. God determines which possibility to become a reality hence the actual reality is predetermined before the hypothetical possibilities. Middle knowledge does not seem to offer any better resolution then Arminianism, and is worse because it perpetuates a soft determinism.

Cook affirms that God's sovereignty is the basis of his absolute knowledge. He also argues middle knowledge and humanity's libertarian free will are compatible. His point may be that God's actual knowledge guarantees that we will choose a specific act but not that we must of necessity so choose to do so. However, this does not reduce the fact that God knows, and because God specifically directs the actual outcome, Molinism

39. See ibid., 96–97.
40. Cook, "God, Middle Knowledge and Alternative Worlds," 302.

comes very close to manipulation. Even so, Cook believes middle knowledge can solve the dilemma of the long debate between Calvinism and Arminianism. The model is more sophisticated, but has it really resolved the dilemma? I think not.

Middle knowledge becomes understandable when one embraces the Arminian concept of human freedom, along with a "soft" Calvinistic determinism. Also, one most likely will maintain the Classical theistic understanding of God as atemporal.

All the above models have problems they cannot resolve. Most importantly, they cannot present a satisfactory account of a dynamic, personal, interactive and interdependent relationship that requires a certain range of authentic freedom for both humanity and the living God.[41] The dramatic biblical presentations of God and human beings' interactive relationship and the very act of "prayer" imply this kind of reality. Yet, the above models exclude such a reality. If "God knows in advance exactly how I will react at each point" how then "can he be said to enter into a genuine interpersonal communication relationship with me."[42] Models based upon Classical theism make prayers of petition and intercession nonsensical because such praying implies that God might do something different then what he might have done. Henry Knight's statement is instructive. He writes, "the claim that such prayers (petition and intercession) have as their only real purpose the disposing of our hearts to receive what God gives and to serve where God directs seems a bit forced; if that's all we mean, why not simply pray that way."[43]

"God's plans call for voluntary cooperation of his creatures." This means that the absolute totality of the future is not decided unilaterally by God or simply by humanity.[44] "How can there possibly be truths and infallible divine beliefs about what I shall freely do far in advance of any

41. I believe the problem arises when the Immanent Trinity (God in relation to Godself apart from creation) takes precedent over and redefines the Economic Trinity (God's revelation to humanity in space-time). I will allow the testimony of God's revelation to humanity as narrated in Scripture to be the beginning and the defining understanding of God.

42. Hasker, "Providence and Evil," 100.

43. Knight, *Future for Truth*, 166.

44. Godfrey Vesey, ed., *The Philosophy in Christianity* (Cambridge: Cambridge University Press, 1989) 130.

deliberation and decision making on my part?"[45] The only possible way to resolve this issue is to present a model that does not argue for absolute knowledge or a fixed unilateral history. Furthermore, the concept of absolute foreknowledge from a Classical theistic view is incompatible with the concept that God interacts with creation on a momentary basis. In order to achieve a genuine human freedom that embraces the dynamic relationship between God and humanity as articulated throughout Scripture, I will present an Open theistic model.

OPEN THEISM

Pentecostals proclaim to have an intimate relationship with the Holy Trinity. This intimate relationship is made possible through the activity of the Holy Spirit. God is a personal being who can enter into dynamic relationship with his creation. Clark Pinnock notes that Pentecostals have helped foster a dynamic relational theism. Pinnock attributes this to Pentecostal "pulpit theology." Pentecostal preachers present the Biblical, narrated portraits of God to the congregation. The biblical narrative speaks about God in the most intimate, relational, personal terms.[46] The living God is moved by what he sees happening, by what he hears, by what he knows. "The fact that God is touched, moved and concerned with us is the very foundation of our hope."[47] Pentecostals declare that God is personal and God is present in history and acting and reacting in time. Pinnock writes, "One of the reasons God has used this movement so mightily is precisely its holy bold witness to the relationality of God."[48]

Open theism articulates an interaction between God and humanity which is a dynamic interrelationship. "When we cease to insist that God already knows the entire course of the future, we can affirm God's genuine interaction with the creaturely world"[49] Therefore, an Openness model

45. Morris, *Our Idea of God*, 97.

46. Clark H. Pinnock, "Divine Relationality: A Pentecostal Contribution to the Doctrine of God," *Journal of Pentecostal Theology* 16 (April 2000) 21.

47. See Samuel Solivan, *The Spirit, Pathos and Liberation: Toward an Hispanic Pentecostal Theology* (Sheffield: Sheffield Academic Press, 1998) 47–77, cited p. 76. I agree with Solivan's statement, "This seeing, hearing and knowing is not anthropomorphic attribution to God. Rather, it rightly reflects a God who shares with us his likeness and image" (p. 75).

48. "Divine Relationality," 21.

49. Godfrey Vesey, *Philosophy in Christianity*, 137.

presents a social triune God as deciding and deliberating in time how God will respond to the temporal actions of his free creatures.[50]

Open theism overcomes the static existence of God and the universe and asserts humans are self-determent agents. It does so by arguing that God is actively involved in every aspect of present creation in a nondeterministic relationship. It accomplishes this by working with a synergistic understanding of salvation and redefining the concept of omniscience.[51] Other concepts of God are also modified in light of this, such as immutability, impassibility and timeless eternity. However, my concern is omniscience.

An Open theistic view of omniscience is presented by Rice. His definition will be my working definition for this model:

> In some respects the future is knowable, in others it is not. God knows a great deal about what will happen. He knows everything that will ever happen as the direct result of factors that already exist . . . he knows the ultimate outcome to which he is guiding the course of history. All that God does not know is the content of future free decisions, and this is because decisions are not there to know until they occur.[52]

Omniscience, then, cannot mean knowing everything but only knowing all that there is to be known. The future free choices to be made cannot be known absolutely because they have not yet transpired. "The past no longer exists except in the omniscience of God. The future exists only as a myriad of possibilities some of which will actually take place."[53] From this perspective, God does not have absolute knowledge of the future. "The future is partly open to God, for God cannot foreknow the decisions that free agents shall make." Further stated, God knows some of the future as settled (his general plans concerning redemption), as well as the

50. William Hasker, "Providence and Evil: Three Theories," *Religious Studies* 21 (1992) 101.

51. See a very helpful paper by Pentecostal theologian Mark D. McLean, "Transcendence and Immanence and the attributes of God" a paper presented to the Twenty Second Annual Meeting of the Society of Pentecostal Studies, Springfield, Missouri, November 12–14, 1992. McLean also finds the classical theistic models unsatisfactory for the practice of Pentecostal prayer and mission.

52. Rice, *Grace of God and the Will of Man*, 134.

53. Mark D. McLean, "Transcendence and Immanence and the Attributes of God" a paper presented to the Twenty Second Annual Meeting of the Society of Pentecostal Studies, Springfield Missouri (November 12–14, 1992) 29.

myriad of possibilities.[54] God leaves us truly free and God remains free to act as God. In this way God is still omniscient. God knows what is knowable. However, "nothing will utterly and fundamentally surprise God . . . and nothing can ultimately thwart his plans because of his power."[55]

The Openness model is usually attacked on two fronts—logically and theologically. It is argued that it is illogical to say God is omniscient without embracing absolute knowledge of past, present and *future*. However, one can argue logically that God is omnipotent, while saying that God cannot or would not create a rock that he cannot lift. God has imposed self-limitations out of his character. Thus, to create a rock he cannot lift is nonsensical.

God does not know the absolute future of free contingent beings because it is philosophically impossible to know what has not yet transpired. Could not God impose self-limitations upon himself? Such limitation creates the necessary space which enables God and humanity (as well as creation) to enjoy authentic interpersonal relationships. The Social Trinity invites us to co-create (in some measure) the future. The future is constrained by the past and present but not determined because it is not yet known. God is the future destiny of all creation; however, the future does not exist in a full sense because it is still under construction.

Secondly, theological concerns are raised in relationship to the understanding of God's providence, especially biblical predictive prophecy. Cook argues against an Openness model by suggesting that God cannot grant guidance to anyone because God cannot know it himself. Yet, contrary to determinism, God's providence is not the unalterable outworking of a predetermined unchangeable plan established in the past eternity. Providence is God's creative response to events as they happen in present space-time based on God's perfect anticipation of the future and his infinite capacity to work for good in every situation according to God's general plan.[56] The Social Trinity's nature as relational dynamic holy-love is constant and consistent; however the future is becoming what may be potentially possible. The Social Trinity's grand plot can be achieved through space-time as the unpredictable mini-plots unfold.

---

54. Beilby and Eddy, *Divine Foreknowledge*, 10. See also the essay by Open theist Gregory Boyd, "Open Theism View," found in the above-mentioned book.

55. Morris, *Our Idea of God*, 101.

56. See Pinnock, *Grace of God and the Will of Man*, 136.

The practical result of an Openness concept of providence is it allows us to acknowledge that we and creation experience some things which are not good for us, not necessarily God's will for our lives. It also helps to solve the problem of evil, for God only allowed evil to be a possibility as a result of creating genuine free moral agents (humans and angels). Therefore, an Openness model offers a better theological response to the problem of evil.[57] I would also add the model is logically consistent and makes better sense out of the biblical presentations of intercessory prayer, than the other models.

Why would it be impossible for God to offer guidance even if God does not possess absolute knowledge of the future? Does not God desire us to develop Christ likeness in character? Virtuous living and Christ like choices are not dependent upon God knowing the future, but are dependent upon our relationship with the Holy Spirit. In other words, a person does not pray to God because God infallibly knows the future, but one prays because the future is not fixed, and God is able to change things.

Some passages of Scripture do speak of future events in specific detail which require a "special" divine intervention. But does this require God to predetermine it or have some absolute foreknowledge in order to bring the event into existence? No. It is possible for the Social Trinity in historical interaction with creation to recognize a possibility, speak forth a specific particle outcome and bring it to pass without having to predetermine the event prior to creation or simply foreseeing the event. I understand the future to be partially open because it has been somewhat constrained. Thus, God in space-time relationship with creation, rebellious humanity, and especially the redeemed covenant community, creates a tomorrow as creation moves toward the coming of God. No doubt it contains disappointments and suffering; yet, we presently have hope in God. Tomorrow is unknowable in every detail, because it does not yet exist. It is imaginable, though, because it is in the creative womb of God's being.

Prophecy functions out of divine activity within the present. Prophecy is not primarily concerned with divine foreknowledge. Prophecy is the result of divine agency. God will act a certain way, or this will come about in a certain way. Thus, God may at times take direct action to bring about the fulfillment of a prophecy uttered within past history. These acts are

57. Morris, *Our Idea of God*, 101.

highly exceptional, yet, available options for God. Divine prophecy does not demand it to be predetermined before creation, or foreseen prior to creation. God in the historical process predicted and brought it to pass. As Rice notes, "It is important to remember that occasional divine intervention is compatible with the affirmation of genuine creaturely freedom, while absolute foreknowledge is not."[58]

It is of immense importance to me that my idea of God corresponds as nearly as possible to the "actual" God as testified to in Scripture. Specifically, it is out of our personal relationship with Jesus Christ—mediated to us by means of the Holy Spirit and in relationship with a Christian community—that we come to better understand the triune God who "knows" us, ever so intimately. God did not predetermine my existence before creation even though the act of creation made it possible for my existence. The Social Trinity, however, was determined to invite, not make, me enter into a redemption relation with God, humanity, and creation. It is a mystery to me that the triune God would enter into the space-time continuum, experience delight and sorrow, pain and pleasure, love and anger, in order to have an authentic relationship with all of creation.

In conclusion, I have attempted to interact with two classical theistic models of God's omniscience and human freedom in order to present an Open theistic model. I believe the Openness model is much more conducive to Pentecostal spirituality and practices. It offers a better theological explanation of the biblical portrayal of the dynamic interactive relationship between God and humanity.

I have presented a model of a personal and relational God who is able to know everything possible (but does not have absolute foreknowledge); who can bring about his general plans of creation, redemption, new creation; who is vulnerable (humanity does frustrate God and God does suffer); and who is presently active in the space-time continuum. God is everlasting (temporal). God is sovereign, yet risks because of self imposed limitations. God reigns with loving wisdom and powerful strength out of a covenant relationship with his creation. God responds, changes his

---

58. Richard Rice, "Divine Foreknowledge and Free-Will Theism," in Clark Pinnock, *The Grace of God and the Will of Man*, 136ff. For other Open theistic ways to account for prophecy, see Boyd's essay Beilby and Eddy, *Divine Foreknowledge*, and Sanders, *God Who Risks*, 131–39.

mind, relents at times from rightful wrath, but will accomplish his plan which includes genuine human freedom.

The Social Trinity has invited us into a dynamic relationship where "genuine dialogue" takes place. Human freedom is understood to be an accountable and responsible gift. God invites us to participate in shaping and, with some limitations, create the future.

I believe that this presentation of God and human freedom is biblically sound, logically valid, and presents the best theodicy. Likewise, Open theism actually achieves what the Arminian model attempts—to affirm a synergistic understanding of salvation that allows for libertarian human responses. But most importantly, I believe the Openness model of a future (which is somewhat determined and somewhat open) best reflects and supports the Pentecostal prayerful engagement of the Almighty God as modeled to us in Scripture.

A CLOSING HYMN: "AWESOME GOD"

Our God is an awesome God;
He reigns from Heaven above with wisdom power and love;
Our God is an awesome God![59]

---

59. Text by Rich Mullins, copyright by BMG songs, 1988.

Excursus[60]

An Extended Review of Graham Old's Essay, "Charismatic Calvinism View"[61]

GRAHAM OLD OPENS HIS essay, "Charismatic Calvinism View," with a clear statement of his primary objective which is to present a Calvinistic model of divine sovereignty and human responsibility.[62] He argues that the Bible presents a sovereign God who determines everything, yet God grants humans the freedom to act in non-coerced ways. In this model, God holds humans responsible for their actions, even though God has predetermined them to act in a certain way. Old argues that these two poles—divine sovereignty and human responsibility—are generated by Scripture. He further states that the "biblical tension" created by these two poles should not be resolved.

Old argues that his concepts of human freedom and a deterministic sovereign God are compatible and illogical. In other words, Old would like to avoid the charge of violating the law of non-contradiction (a philosophical means of validating a truth claim by demonstrating that the system of thought is coherent in its argument). He consistently affirms that God has predetermined everything that transpires; yet, he simultane-

60. The editors of *Pneuma Review* sponsored a dialogue addressing three different theological views concerning God's knowledge. The three views presented were an Open theistic view, Charismatic Calvinistic view and an Arminian view. Each panelist presented his position and then was given opportunity to respond to the other two positions. The essays and responses were published between 2002 and 2004. *Pneuma Review* targets pastors and laity from the Pentecostal and Charismatic traditions. I presented the Open theistic view. Graham Old presented a classical Calvinistic view.

61. Graham Old, "Charismatic Calvinism View," *Pneuma Review* 5 (2002) 47–57; hereafter Old's essay will be referred to as CCV.

62. For a introduction to Calvinism, see H. Henry Meeter, revised by Paul A Marshal, *The Basic Ideas of Calvinism*, sixth ed. (Grand Rapids: Baker, 1990) 15–23.

ously affirms that humans in their present daily affairs of life "freely" make choices.

Old correctly asserts that Calvinists believe God has an intimate relationship with humanity. This refreshingly brief affirmation, however, is drowned out by the deafening theme of God's sovereignty. Sovereignty is the controlling metaphor of God's nature in Calvinism. Sovereignty is the "fundamental principle" that coherently holds the whole theological system together. In Calvinism, sovereignty simply means God has predetermined everything and providentially sees that it comes to pass. God's sovereign will is the ultimate and effectual cause of all that happens, as John Calvin made clear. Calvin wrote,

> we make God ruler and governor of all things, who in accordance with his wisdom has from the farthest limit of eternity decreed what he was going to do, and now by his might carries out what he has decreed.[63]

Sovereignty, in other words, is simply affirming that "everything is controlled by God's secret purpose, and nothing can happen except by his knowledge and will. . . . [and] that every event comes from his intended will. . . . because nothing happens without his order or permission."[64] God does not actually allow or permit things to happen because God has already determined what will happen. Therefore every event that transpires is God's premeditated intention.

With Calvin and Old, I agree that sovereignty requires God to be intimately involved with all of creation. However, I cannot accept the argument that sovereignty must be defined in such a manner that one must logically conclude, "that nothing can happen unless he [God] ordered it."[65] In the Calvinistic model, everything that happens is a direct result of God's will—the so-called "secret working" of God's eternal immutable decree.

In his essay, Old attempts to portray human freedom and deterministic sovereignty as being compatible. He is unable to pull it off. He does

---

63. John T. McNeill, ed., *Calvin: Institutes of Christian Religion* (Philadelphia: Westminster) 207.

64. Tony Lane and Hilary Osborne, eds., *John Calvin: The Institutes of Christian Religion* (Grand Rapids: Baker, 1987) 72, 73, 75. The following quotations will be from this addition.

65. Ibid, 81. Calvin saw his Christian view of determinism to be very comforting.

not explain how predeterminism and free will are compatible. Instead he asserts that they are non-contradictory and then turns to Scripture to support his statement. He seems to believe that if he can show that Scripture supports his belief that God predetermines everything, and that biblical characters seem to think they have free will, then we should accept it. What Old offers the readers is a Calvinistic explanation of Scripture.[66]

Old is not able to reasonably explain the relationship between a deterministic sovereign God and humans who are free to make choices. When it comes to explaining the relationship between a deterministic God and human freedom, he makes the typical Calvinistic move: it is a mystery beyond comprehension.[67] But is it really a mystery and humanly incomprehensible? I do not think so. Where is the mystery? If God has predetermined everything and providentially sees that it is fulfilled, then what is mysterious? The mystery must be that it violates the law of non-contradiction.

Old writes, once we "accept that 'it is possible for God to predestine an act to come to pass *by means* of the deliberate choices of individuals' a whole host of texts suddenly make sense."[68] He states we must simply accept it because this is what the Bible tells us. But the *Bible* is not simply telling us this. Rather, he is explaining the Scripture. If you accept his presupposition that God has predetermined everything (past, present and future) then I suppose you would "make sense" out of the Bible from his viewpoint. But the "making of sense" would be from a Calvinistic theological position. The Bible is now filtered through the lens of Calvinism. However, the challenge is that other Christians, who take Scripture just as serious and are not Calvinists, would not explain these texts from his theological perspective.[69] This is why theologians turn to other means to support their theological positions. Scripture is always foundational, but

66. For an Open theistic explanation of the most pertinent so-called deterministic passages of Scripture see Gregory A. Boyd, *God of the Possible: A Biblical Introduction to the Open View of God* (Grand Rapids: Baker, 2000).

67. CCV, 54 and see his footnote 13. Also see the references made it my essay on Open Theism in *Pneuma Review* 5 (2002).

68. CCV, 54 (emphasis his).

69. Historically speaking, this would include most of the Patristic Fathers, Eastern Orthodoxy, Arminians, Wesleyans, and Pentecostals. We should remember that in the sixteenth century, Calvinism was the newest theological idea. I think we need to set aside the myth that the Bible alone can resolve all the various doctrinal differences that exist among Christians.

never alone, and never free from presuppositions that shape the development of their doctrine.

Graham Old wants to avoid the charge made by Arminians, Wesleyans, and Open theists that the Calvinistic definition of sovereignty precludes any authentic human choice.[70] To state it differently, he wants to avoid the charge that his definition of sovereignty contradicts the definition of humans having freedom to make non-coerced choices.[71]

Old is clear about his definition of human freedom. He explicitly defines human freedom. People make choices according to their strongest internal desire. One could hypothetically ask, "Can a person do something that is contrary to God's will?" According to Old's model, the answer would have to be an emphatic no. Why? Because God places the "strongest internal desire" in the person's heart, therefore guaranteeing that God's will is done.[72] On the other hand, he is not as clear about his definition of sovereignty. He defines sovereignty as "God intentionally ordaining, and using, the intentional actions of human beings to bring about his good purpose."[73]

These definitions, as used by Calvinists and determinists, are simply incompatible and inherently contradictory—the very thing that Old desired to avoid. I would rather Old move away from his dependence upon philosophical rationalism (law of non-contradiction) and simply assert that it is contradictory and incompatible.[74] The acceptance of intellectual rationalism and the adaptation of philosophical determinism, reworked in the biblical language of sovereignty, creates significant problems for the biblical presentation that humans have a free will. A Calvinistic model of God's sovereignty makes it impossible for authentic human freedom to exist no matter how complex and sophisticated the argument.

Back to Calvin, he wrote,

if only we had eyes to see, we would realize that the glory of his [Christ Jesus] Father shines out in this situation. We must have

70. For a historically informed and very readable explanation of a Wesleyan presentation of theology that addresses the Arminian and Calvinistic understanding of God's knowledge see Milder Bangs Wynkoop, *Foundations of Wesleyan-Arminian Theology* (Kansas City, MO: Beacon Hill, 1967).

71. CCV, 58.

72. Ibid.

73. Ibid., and see *John Calvin*, 75–82.

74. I would suggest that this might be a more "charismatic" Calvinistic model.

humility, not compelling God to render an account, but so acknowledging his hidden purposes that we recognize his will must be best.[75]

This portrait may be comforting for John Calvin and Calvinists in general,[76] but I personally find it disturbing. The Calvinistic view of God's will must state that all the evil atrocities humans commit, such as the Holocaust, abortions, rapes, murders, slavery, and terrorist activity are the will of God. In Old's model of God's sovereignty, things would not or could not happen if God did not will it (predestine it).[77] Why would God decree such horrific evils? For Calvinists it is always for God's glory, the unquestionable and hidden purpose.

The problem of evil is a concern that all Christian traditions address.[78] But, for the Calvinistic model this problem is acute. They assert that what happens is always God's will. In fairness, Calvinists would never state that those who commit such evils should go unpunished or that workers of iniquity should say what happened was God's will, thus avoiding personal responsibility.[79] Calvinists would argue that individuals must be held accountable for their actions. No doubt, this is an important reason for Calvinists to attempt to demonstrate that predeterminism and human freedom is compatible.

Some Christian traditions have addressed the problem of evil, human freedom, and divine sovereignty by appropriating biblical concepts such as God's *perfect* will and God's *permissive* will. This makes sense of those passages that say God was grieved, or humans have grieved the Holy Spirit.[80] In Calvinism, however, there is no distinction between perfect and permissive will. Whatever happens is always the sovereign will of God.

The Calvinistic model does not articulate a difference between God *allowing* something to happen and God *causing* something to happen. A Calvinist cannot logically say God permitted something to happen. Why,

75. *John Calvin*, 76, and CCV, 65.

76. *John Calvin*, 71.

77. CCV, 64.

78. For an Open Theistic view that is also charismatic, see Gregory A. Boyd, *Satan and the Problem of Evil: Constructing A Trinitarian Warfare Theodicy* (Downers Grove, IL: InterVarsity, 2001).

79. See *John Calvin*, 77.

80. See Gen 6:6 and Eph 4:30.

because God determined it to happen. Therefore everything that happens is God's perfect will. For Old, God is *the* cause, the ultimate and necessary cause of all that happens. It must be this way because of how Calvinists define sovereignty.

In the discussion on human freedom, Graham Old explicitly defines and then takes time to explain how human freedom is compatible with God determining human activity. However, he does not explicitly define and explain his concept of sovereignty. Sovereignty, will, and purpose seem to function as synonyms in this essay. However, from his essay I think it would be fair to say that sovereignty is God's intentional ordering of all events.[81] Furthermore, sovereignty is understood as "God himself planning ahead a certain course of action" which all of creation will follow.[82] I think he would agree that sovereignty means that God has orchestrated everything that has or ever will happen, right down to the minutest detail. This would even include those who will or will not become Christian.[83]

For those of us who are not determinists, we see the inherent contradiction between predeterminism and human freedom. The argument for predeterminism and human freedom is circular and contradictory. If God has predetermined what will happen then humans really must do what God has predetermined. Are humans really capable of making free choices? Calvinists say, "Yes!" They offer a lengthy argument that people do make free choices based on their strongest internal desire—desire that comes directly from God. From the perspective of non-Calvinistic Christians, the Calvinistic reasonable argument is illogical and contradictory. Furthermore, the Calvinistic model makes God directly responsible for everything (even evil), thus tarnishing His glory, and contradicting portions of Scripture.[84]

I have personally performed funerals of children. It is very difficult for me to swallow the idea that it is God's will for them to die at this stage of life. What comfort comes from a notion that it was God's will that one's spouse be brutally raped, or be consumed in a towering inferno? How do we reconcile the reality that many children are starving from hunger today with the biblical portrait of God being concerned for the orphans,

81. CCV, 53.

82. Ibid.

83. See my "response to readers," *Pneuma Review* 6 (2003) 60–64 for further discussion.

84. As seems clear through the entire book of Genesis.

widows, and poor? Old responds it is according with God's will that such things happen because "life and death, riches and poverty, shame and honour come from the Lord."[85]

Romans 8:28 states, "We know that all things work together for the good of those who love God, who are called according to his purpose."[86] It is one thing to say that God can work all things out according to his purpose, if we understand purpose to be an overarching sovereignty that allows for a limited freedom for volitional beings. It is something else to say everything that happens is God purposefully working out his predetermined sovereign will. I believe God can use any event, whether good or bad, to shape my character and continue to transform me into the image of his Son. God is sovereign and he does *allow* evil to manifest and may even send hardships my way.[87] However, I disagree that every event that happens is God's "perfect" will.

An important implication of the Calvinistic concept of sovereignty has to do with how we understand God's knowledge. When we discuss God's knowledge we generally relate it to how we experience time. We say that God *foreknew* when we talk about the future, and we say that God *knew* when we talk about the past. In this way Old discusses God's knowledge from the perspective of our human experience of time.[88] Old does explain from a Calvinistic perspective *how* God has arrived at or comes to possess knowledge. "God knows the future because he has planned it."[89] He is correct when he says that Arminians believe that God's plans are based upon foreknowledge. God foresaw how humans respond to certain things. For Arminians, however, this explanation of *how* God knows the future is significantly different. For Calvinists, God does not foresee the future: God has determined the future. Therefore, in Calvinism, God's knowledge comes from him predetermining events, not foreseeing how humans would respond to certain situations.

I think that Graham Old needs to offer further explanation on how God knows what he knows. This is the pivotal issue in the whole debate about human freedom and God's sovereignty. I would, also, like him to

85. CCV, 54.
86. NRSV.
87. As seems obvious to me from many passages throughout the book of Hebrews.
88. CCV, 62.
89. Ibid., 64.

explain how his Calvinistic model does not collapse into some static existence of God. To say that God is affected and to give a list of Reformed theologians who say such things are insufficient.[90] What is needed is an explanation on how his model can accommodate such assertions. How does Calvinism avoid the logical conclusion that God is always the active agent and humans are simply passive instruments? It is not enough to assert that God responds and God is not static. One must demonstrate the validity of the statement as it pertains to the model being advocated. Graham Old needs to demonstrate and explain how his model of God can incorporate temporality and change, those things which are requirements for authentic response. The classical philosophical doctrines called immutability and impassability that traditional Calvinism has embraced do not allow for a non-static God who responds to his creation in God's present interaction in space-time. I do realize that this may go beyond the initial concerns of his essay.

Old cites Grudem saying God is influenced by what humans do. How does this affect God and God's will? God has already determined it, thus, through personal providence, he carries out what will happen. From our existence in time we would say God decided in the past what will transpire in the future. The decision had been finalized. To suggest that God is influenced and reacts to humans presently may appear to soften God, or even make the model more biblically palatable. But, it really does not help resolve the logical consequences of the model. Millard Erickson, who is a staunch advocate of the Classical theistic model writes, "God is timeless.... He has always been what he is."[91] Erickson further writes, "He has from all eternity determined what he is now doing. Thus his actions are not in any sense reactions or developments."[92] "God does not change his mind, plans or actions, for these rest upon his nature, which remains unchanged no matter what happens."[93] The traditional Calvinistic model has no room in it for a God who is affected, without first predetermining how He is affected.

90. The listing of names of respected theologians reminds me of the early Fundamentalists and Modernists debates of the 1920's. I think what it shows is that there are many academically trained Christian theologians who love God and yet differ greatly in how they understand God. Drawing up lists will not resolve the differences.

91. Millard J. Erickson, *Christian Theology* (Grand Rapids: Baker, 1985) 274.

92. Ibid., 275

93. Ibid, 278.

The Calvinistic Deterministic model of sovereignty has important overtones for one's understanding of soteriology (the doctrine of salvation). From the Calvinistic perspective God has predestined who will or will not be saved; not by foreseeing their future choice (Arminianism) or through his prevenient grace that creates an opportunity to freely accept or reject salvation (Wesleyanism).[94] In Calvinism, it is because of his sovereign glory.[95] Calvinism holds that God has predetermined who will be saved. The elect experience saving grace which is irresistible. The elect are saved and the rest of humanity is damned the hell. This view of salvation is called monergism. God determines who will be saved and God does all the work to save them, hence, grace is irresistible. Monergist's like Old may say that the person freely rejected the Gospel invitation, but he already made clear in his essay that humans do exactly what God places in their heart.

In Calvinism, God does not foresee, God determines. In making his sovereign choice God has determined who will receive the atoning sacrifice for salvation—limited to the "individuals" who were predetermined to be saved. Thus, Jesus's death was for the elect individuals and not for "whosoever calls upon the name of the Lord."[96] The elect individual responds to the Gospel because of the "internal desire" placed there by God.

Arminians, Wesleyans, Pentecostals and Open theists would argue that it is God's will for all to be saved; yet we realize that people reject the Gospel invitation due to their own resistance to God's gracious invitation. ("The Lord . . . is longsuffering to toward us, not willing that any should perish, but all should come to repentance." 2 Peter 3:9 NKJV). This would be a synergistic understanding of salvation. A biblical synergistic understanding affirms that God always initiates the redemptive relationship which enables the depraved person the ability to respond our reject God's grace. Salvation is by grace through faith. One never earns God's grace because of human effort. However, God's grace is resistible! When people resist God they grieve the Holy Spirit.

94. See Henry H. Knight III, "Love and Freedom (By Grace Alone) in Wesley's Soteriology: A Proposal for evangelicals," *Pneuma* 24 (2002) 57–67.

95. For an overview of John Calvin and his theology, see Timothy George, *Theology of the Reformers* (Nashville: Broadman, 1988) chapter 5 titled, "Glory Unto God: John Calvin," 163–251.

96. See Rom 10:13, John 3, and 1 John 5.

For the Calvinists, people are not saved because God did not place the necessary internal desire in their heart or send the grace necessary to convert them. Stated differently, those who do respond, do so because God picked them (his sovereign choice from eternity past) and then predestined them for salvation. People do not have a choice, they must respond to God's irresistible grace positively. For monergists like Calvin, this is the logical extension of God's sovereignty. For synergists, like the early Pentecostal leader William Seymour, monergism is incompatible with the overarching biblical portrait of the character of a loving God who sent the Son to save all who call upon his name.

I appreciated Graham Old's desire to be faithful to his Calvinistic tradition while allowing his charismatic experiences of the Spirit to reshape it. In reality, Graham Old's "charismatic" model is not necessarily a new twist on the traditional Calvinistic model concerning God's will or knowledge. His "charismatic" model does not really change the monergistic and deterministic theological system of Calvinism. Calvinists, generally speaking, emphasize God's providential involvement with all of creation—an intimate deterministic relationship. I would assume that by referring to himself as charismatic, he would no longer be a cessationist concerning the gifts of the Spirit (which is a *significant* amendment to traditional Calvinism). However, he still remains a staunch apologist for a large conservative group in the Reformed tradition. Readers and theologians will probably question his belief that his charismatic Calvinistic model of God "fits perfectly" into a Pentecostal model of God.[97]

97. As a classical Pentecostal, I have some concerns about Old's opening statement of his essay. He states that his charismatic Calvinistic model "fits perfectly within a Pentecostal/charismatic understanding of God." This raises various issues concerning the definition of Pentecostalism, Pentecostal identity, and the historic emergence of Pentecostalism and the charismatic movement. I do not think Graham Old would want to be classified as a classical or even a contemporary Pentecostal. He would rather understand his theological tradition as "charismatic" Calvinist. He is representing the Reformed tradition. It is important to remember that historically Pentecostalism has been Wesleyan and Arminian in its theological orientation not Calvinistic. All classical Pentecostal denominations, whether they were more Wesleyan or more Baptistic in their theological persuasion, rejected Calvinism as a theological system. Therefore to suggest it fits perfectly into a Pentecostal model is problematic for a classical Pentecostal. It seems for Old the terms Pentecostal and charismatic are synonyms. Maybe it would be better to differentiate between Pentecostal and charismatic. Pentecostal is a noun which refers to a distinct theological community and theological system. Charismatic is an adjective which modifies an existing theological system (Calvinism, Lutheranism, Catholic, etc). Old is a Calvinist but because of his experience of the Spirit would consider himself as a

As I read Old's essay, I was reminded of my dear Calvinistic friend, who has passed away. He was a graduate of Westminster and a five point Calvinist. We were ministering in the same town. This was my first pastorate and I was young. He was about forty years older than me. He was a seasoned minister, and I was the rookie. We became good friends. Many times we came together to read Scripture, debate theological views, and discuss pastoral problems, but the most memorable were those times we came together to pray. Even though we had held to different theological positions (he was a staunch five point Calvinist and cessationist), we both believed in Christian fellowship and prayer. I say this because I do not want the readers to think that I am insinuating that Calvinists (or monergists in general) do not pray. They are compassionate ministers who pray with the parishioners. From my perspective, the fact that they offer petitionary prayers should obligate them to modify their model of God not simply affirm that it is God's will that they pray.[98]

In summary, let me say that I appreciated his fine essay, which was clearly presented and biblically engaging. I would like Graham Old to offer an explanation of the relationship of sovereignty and knowledge and how this impacts human freedom. I also would appreciate clarification of what he means by *will*, *purposes*, and *sovereignty*. Finally, I would like to suggest that he give up trying to demonstrate the compatibility of deterministic sovereignty and human freedom because in the end it is not compatible. Contrary to his assertions, this incompatibility exists not because of how non-Calvinists define human freedom, but because of how Calvinists define God's sovereignty. Furthermore, the notion of monergism, which affirms total depravity of humanity and God as the deterministic cause, has no logical pause in the order of salvation for personal freedom of response—a response that would resist God's grace.

I pray that the Lord will give us all more opportunities to listen to those Christians who may have different beliefs and practices. I can certainly testify that I have benefited spiritually from my long-term relationship with Christians from various theological persuasions. May the Lord God help us all to love one another even as we disagree over important theological concerns. To God be the Glory, Amen!

---

charismatic Calvinist. From this perspective we affirm a shared common experience in the Spirit, yet remain a part of our distinct theological communities.

98. See Clark H. Pinnock, *Most Moved Mover: A Theology of God's Openness* (Grand Rapids: Baker, 2000).

6

The Spirit and Theological Interpretation

A Pentecostal Strategy

The Bible's meaning for today cannot result automatically from the correct use of a set of hermeneutical principles.[1]

—Richard Bauckham

Pentecostals . . . would want to approach interpretation as a matter of the text, the community, and also the ongoing voice of the Holy Spirit.[2]

—Rickie Moore

THE THEOLOGICAL INTERPRETIVE STRATEGY being presented embraces a dialogical interdependent relationship between the Holy Spirit, Christianity's sacred Scriptures, and an actual ecclesiastical narrative tradition in the hermeneutical process of the making of meaning. The readers in community, the Bible, and the Holy Spirit are interdependent dialogical partners participating in a tridactic negotiation for theological meaning. The theological interpretive strategy being proposed emerged from Pentecostal praxis and theological engagement with Scripture and the Spirit. Thus, the strategy is a product of an ecclesiastical narrative tradition—a Pentecostal community. However, as a strategy for theological interpretation, it may not be unique to Pentecostalism; furthermore, I believe that as a strategy for theological interpretation it could be beneficial to other Christian traditions.

---

1. *The Bible in Politics: How to Read the Bible Politically* (Louisville: Westminster John Knox, 1989) 19.

2. "Canon and Charisma in the Book of Deuteronomy," *Journal of Pentecostal Theology* 1 (1992) 75–92.

The theological strategy affirms the important contributions that the Holy Spirit and Pentecostal community bring to the interpretive process. As a result, there will be a shift from the more modernistic emphasis on the individual hermeneut and *his* commitment to an acceptable and correctly applied scientific method of biblical interpretation to a primary emphasis upon the Christian community as the context through which interpretation takes place.[3] The community's story is the primary filter through which interpretation takes place.[4]

The strategy does not pretend to be a full-blown theory of interpretation, nor will it desire to become a static methodological procedure. Nevertheless, the strategy is a product of a Christian community and based upon the biblical model of Acts 15, the Jerusalem Council.[5] The hermeneutic is conversational in nature and embraces a tridactic negotiation for theological meaning. The Bible, the Holy Spirit, and the Pentecostal community are actively engaging each other in the conversation. Meaning, then, is arrived at through a dialectical process based upon an interdependent dialogical relationship between Scripture, Spirit, and community.

This tridactic conversational approach to "meaning" is necessary because all forms of communication are underdeterminate; that is, a listener or reader is needed to complete the communicative event, hence participating in the production of meaning.[6] This does not imply that the

3. "His" is used purposefully to reiterate the male dominance of Enlightenment interpretation that has argued for a scientific neutral and objective method of interpretation.

4. See Alasdair Macintyre, *After Virtue: A Study in Moral Theory*, 2nd ed. (Notre Dame, IN: University of Notre Dame Press, 1984). Also see MacIntyre's sequel, *Whose Justice? Which Rationality* (Notre Dame, Indiana: University of Notre Dame Press, 1988). MacIntyre's primary concern has been to demonstrate that "dramatic narrative is the crucial form for an understanding of human action" and moral reasoning. Alasdair MacIntyre, "Epistemological Crises, Dramatic Narrative, and the Philosophy of Science" in *Why Narrative? Readings in Narrative Theology*, eds. Stanley Hauerwas and L. Gregory Jones (Grand Rapids: Eerdmans, 1989) 150.

5. See John Christopher Thomas, "Women, Pentecostals and the Bible: An Experiment in Pentecostal Hermeneutics," *Journal of Pentecostal Theology* 5 (1994) 17–40. This hermeneutic is based upon Acts 15, the Jerusalem Council, which is comprised of three primary components in the theological discerning process. These components are the believing community, the activity of the Holy Spirit and Scripture

6. For the concept of "underdeterminate," see Stephen E. Fowl, *Engaging Scripture: A Model for Theological Interpretation* (Malden, MA: Blackwell, 1998) 10. See also J. Severino Croatto, *Biblical Hermeneutics: Toward a Theory of Reading as the Production of Meaning* (Maryknoll, NY: Orbis, 1987), for the notion of the "production of meaning."

biblical passage can mean whatever a community wants or desires it to mean. The written passage does offer guidance and resistance to the readers. There is a dialectical interdependent relationship between the written text and the community of readers. Thus, there exists an actual communication event that takes place, as the text is read/heard. The text, which in this case is a biblical passage, desires to be understood by the readers in a Christian community.[7]

The biblical passage is at the mercy of the community. However, a Christian community should give the biblical passage the opportunity to interact with the readers in such a way that the passage fulfills its dialogical role in the communicative event. This would be the case for the Pentecostal community because she recognizes the Bible as the penultimate authoritative written testimony of Divine revelation—the inspired word of God. Furthermore, the community believes that the Spirit's inspirational relation with Scripture can cause it to speak clearly and creatively as Word of God to the contemporary Pentecostal community's situations and needs. Hence, the Pentecostal community will read the Bible as sacred Scripture that speaks to the community's current needs, thus enabling the community to live faithfully before and with the living God.

The theological strategy is self-consciously a *narrative* approach to the understanding and the making of theological meaning. I am referring to narrative in two ways: (1) as an overarching theological category, and (2) as a method for biblical interpretation. Narrative as a theological category is a way of grasping and making sense of the whole of God's inspired authoritative witness—Scripture.[8] By this I mean to highlight the importance of understanding Scripture as a grand meta-narrative with the Gospels and Acts as the heart of the Christian story. The Social Trinity is the central figure of Christianity, with Jesus Christ being the very heart of the story; therefore a narrative theology will emphasize the priority

---

7. Stephen E. Fowl and L. Gregory Jones, *Reading In Communion: Scripture and Ethics in Christian Life* (Grand Rapids: Eerdmans, 1991) 8.

8. For an informative explanation of the significance of Narrative as a theological category for the understanding of Scripture, see Joel B. Green, "The (Re-) Turn To Narrative," in *Narrative Reading, Narrative Preaching: Reuniting New Testament Interpretation and Proclamation*, eds. Joel B. Green and Michael Pasquarello (Grand Rapids: Baker Academic, 2003) 1–36.

of the Gospel of Jesus Christ and its significance for the Christian community and the world.[9]

The Pentecostal narrative reading strategy is a "text centered" and "reader oriented" interpretive method.[10] Knowledge, as meaningful understanding, will be rooted in and related to human life because "the only sort of [theological and theoretical] knowledge that really counts is knowledge grounded in life."[11] "Meaning, therefore, is no longer seen in terms of an original 'cause' or ultimate 'effect' but in terms of relationship."[12] This meaning is arrived at through a dialectical process based upon an interdependent dialogical relationship between Scripture, Spirit, and community.

The possibility of humans misunderstanding texts and resisting the Spirit further complicates the interpretive process. Hence, John Goldingay's warning should be heeded—"those who pretend to be objective and critical and then find their own concerns in the texts they study need to take a dose of self-suspicion."[13] Interpreters must practice a "hermeneutic of suspicion" and a "hermeneutic of retrieval"[14] as they negotiate creative and constructive meaningful readings of Scripture grounded in the Pentecostal community's desire to live faithfully with God. In the remain-

9. Gerard Loughlin, *Telling God's Story: Bible, Church and Narrative Theology* (Cambridge: Cambridge University Press, 1996) preface. See also his essay, "The Basis and Authority of Doctrine," in *The Cambridge Companion to Doctrine*, ed. Colin E. Gunton (Cambridge: Cambridge University Press, 1997) 41–64, esp. 52–54.

10. Edgar V. McKnight, *Post-Modern Use of the Bible: The Emergence of Reader-Oriented Criticism* (Nashville: Abingdon, 1988). According to McKnight, "The postmodern perspective which allows readers to use the Bible today is that of a radical reader-oriented literary criticism, a criticism which views literature in terms of readers and their values, attitudes, and responses. . . . A *radical* reader-oriented criticism is postmodern in that it challenges the critical assumption that a disinterested reader can approach a text objectively and obtain verifiable knowledge by applying certain scientific strategies. A radical reader-oriented approach sees the strategies, the criteria for criticism and verification, the 'information' obtained by the process, and the use of such 'information' in light of the reader," 14–15.

11. McKnight, *Post-Modern Use of the Bible*, 19.

12. Ibid., 22–23.

13. John Goldingay, *Models for Interpretation of Scripture* (Grand Rapids: Eerdmans, 1995) 45.

14. Paul Ricoeur, *Freud and Philosophy: An Essay on Interpretations* (New Haven: Yale University Press, 1970). Ricoeur argues that "Hermeneutics seems to me to be animated by this double motivation: willingness to suspect, willingness to listen; *vow of rigor, vow of obedience*," 27.

der of this paper I will outline this theological interpretive strategy that embraces a tridactic negotiation for meaning between the biblical text, the Holy Spirit and a Pentecostal (or Christian) community.[15]

THE CONTRIBUTION OF THE BIBLICAL TEXT

In order for a communicative event to take place there must be space between a text; a stable but under-determinate entity; and a reader in community. The reader in community interprets the written text in an attempt to understand the text, thereby completing the communicative act. Semiotics is a theory that emphasizes both the space between the reader and a text and the necessary dialogical and dialectical relationship between the reader and the text in the production of meaning.

Semiotics

Semiotics is concerned with the study of signs as conveyers of meaning.[16] Signs are not limited to a written language but include a great diversity of human (and animal) activities.[17] The focus here, however, is with written communication. Semiotics, as it relates to linguistics,[18] is concerned with both the "speech-act," whether written or spoken, and the "language" in which the speech act functions. Abrams writes that the aim of semiotics "is to regard the *parole* (a single verbal utterance, or particular use of a sign or set of signs) as only a manifestation of the *langue* (that is, the general system implicit differentiations and rules of combination which

15. Current articles dealing with Pentecostal hermeneutics with additional biblio-graphical resources are Kenneth J. Archer, "Pentecostal Hermeneutics: Retrospect and Prospect," *Journal of Pentecostal Theology* 8 (April 1996) 63–81; Veli-Matti Karkkainen, "Pentecostal Hermeneutics in the Making: On the Way from Fundamentalism to Postmodernism," *Journal of the European Pentecostal Theological Association* 18 (1998) 76–115; see also *The Spirit and Church* 2 (2000) which is dedicated to the topic Pentecostal Hermeneutics.

16. Terence Hawkes, *Structuralism and Semiotics* (Berkeley: University of California Press, 1977) 124. Hawkes points out that Europeans prefer semiology in regards to Saussure's coinage of the term whereas English speakers prefer semiotics because of Peirce.

17. See Hawkes, *Structuralism and Semiotics*, chapter 4 for an introduction, explanation and the diversity of Semiotics.

18. M. H. Abrams, *A Glossary of Literary Terms: Seventh Edition* (Orlando: Harcourt Brace, 1999) 280.

underlie and make possible a particular use of signs)."[19] In other words the language (*langue*) "is a system of signs and laws regulating grammar and syntax—a sort of 'canon' establishing guidelines for meaning."[20] Meaning in the sense of what a "speech-act" is saying grammatically is not viewed as a referential sign about what it is referring to historically.[21] Speech (*parole*) "is the *act* executing the given possibilities residing within a system of signs."[22] In order for communication to transpire, both the writer/speaker and the reader/listener must have some competency in the language (*langue*). Therefore, Semiotics emphasizes the transaction of meaning between texts and readers, thus, involving the reader in the production of meaning in order to complete the communication event.

The Bible is a collection of written speech acts. Semiotics, therefore, can provide helpful insights and guidance for a theological hermeneutical strategy which appreciates the formational potential of texts. I do not want to confuse Semiotics with theological or even biblical hermeneutics. Instead I desire to approach a Pentecostal hermeneutical strategy through Semiotics[23] because Semiotics recognizes the necessary distance between the reader and the text by emphasizing the important contributions of both the text and reader in the making of meaning. This space between the reader and text creates a real conversation. Therefore a Semiotic interpretive strategy will be the most conducive for Pentecostals (and I would suggest Christians) because it allows for an open interdependent dialectic interaction between the text and the reading community in the making of meaning. However, the Holy Scripture in its final canonical form provides the primary arena in which the Pentecostal community desires to understand God.[24]

19. Abrams, *Glossary of Literary Terms*, 280.

20. J. Severino Croatto, *Biblical Hermeneutics: Toward a Theory of Reading as Production of Meaning* (Maryknoll, NY: Orbis, 1987) 13.

21. Paul Ricoeur, "Biblical Hermeneutics," *Semeia* 4 (1975) 81.

22. Croatto, *Biblical Hermeneutics*, 14. See also Abrams, *Glossary of Literary Terms*, 141. The distinction between language (a system of signs) and speech was introduced by Saussure.

23. I am following Croatto's argument in *Biblical Hermeneutics*, 10.

24. See J. Barton, *Reading the Old Testament* (Philadelphia: Westminster, 1984) which argues that Brevard Childs' "Canonical Criticism" resembles the principles of New Criticism, 140–57. For a helpful explanation and critique of Brevard Childs' canonical approach, see Charles J. Scalise, *Hermeneutics as Theological Prolegomena: A Canonical Approach* (Macon, GA: Mercer University Press, 1994). Scalise modifies Childs' approach

From a Semiotic viewpoint the text contains latent but nonetheless potent cues as to how it desires to be understood. The way to "see" and "hear" these cues is through a close (formalistic) analysis of the text illuminated by the social cultural context in which it was written. The Pentecostal hermeneutic would affirm the importance of the genre of the passage along with the grammatical rules of the language to which the specific speech-act belongs. The text would be analyzed, however, from a more formalistic perspective while affirming the importance of the social cultural context in which the text came into existence. Meaning is negotiated through the conversation between the text, community, and the Spirit. The world behind the text informs but does not control the conversation.[25]

In short, Semiotics affirms that a dialectical interdependent link exists between the text and the readers. Semiotics also views the text as an under-determinate yet stable entity that affirms the reader as a necessary component in the communicative event and the making of meaning. The text is to be respected as a dialogical partner in the communicative event. Thus semiotics is a helpful critical aspect of theological interpretation.

THE CONTRIBUTION OF A PENTECOSTAL (ECCLESIASTICAL) COMMUNITY

Moral reasoning is always rooted in a particular narrative tradition.[26] Interpretative methods and readings are dependent upon a hermeneutical community. In the negotiating of meaning, one's community is an important and necessary component of the hermeneutic.[27] In order to produce a "Pentecostal" reading of Scripture, one's identity must be shaped by the Pentecostal community.

---

by addressing Childs' inadequate account of tradition and canonical intentionality, and the need to include within a canonical approach newer sociological and literary approach.

25. W. Randolph Tate, *Biblical Interpretation: An Integrated Approach*, rev. ed. (Peabody, MA: Hendrickson, 1997) xxv.

26. See footnote 4 above.

27. See Harry S. Stout, "Theological Commitment and American Religious History," *Theological Education* 25 (1989) 44–59, who demonstrates that there is an inescapable relationship between the community of which one belongs and the explanation of past history. His argument can be extended to include biblical meaning.

I recognize that all interpretive readings are culturally dependent and inherently contain the ideological perspective(s) of the community. Furthermore, both the interpretive method and the community readings are anchored into particular socio-cultural modes of existence. Hermeneutical approaches reflect the socio-theological perspectives of those using them. This ecclesiastical strategy affirms this reality, thus the importance of practicing a hermeneutic of suspicion and retrieval.[28] Also, this strategy affirms a praxis-oriented hermeneutical stance because the interpretive activity is generated in the present concrete experience of living in the Pentecostal community that is animated by the Holy Spirit. The community moves towards the biblical text with specific concerns and needs. The community expects the Scripture(s) to speak to its present situation. The community also listens for the voice of the Spirit and looks for the signs of the Spirit as it engages conversationally with Scripture.

AN ECCLESIASTICAL HERMENEUTICAL COMMUNITY: A PENTECOSTAL COMMUNITY

The Pentecostal theologian must be entrenched within a Pentecostal community and in tune with the concrete needs and aspirations of the Pentecostal community.[29] This strategy affirms the necessity of the hermeneut living among the Pentecostal community. Therefore, the hermeneutical emphasis will fall upon a Semiotic and Narrative approach with the context of the reader in community providing the hermeneutical filter and foil for understanding and completing the communicative event.[30]

The Pentecostal hermeneut who is educated by the academy must also be a participant within the Pentecostal community; that is, she should understand her Christian identity to be Pentecostal. In order to be included as part of the Pentecostal community, she must embrace the

28. See Sandra M. Schneiders, "Feminist Hermeneutics," in *Hearing the New Testament: Strategies for Interpretation*, ed. Joel Green (Grand Rapids: Eerdmans, 1995). Schneiders writes, "Those who continue to hope that the biblical text is susceptibly of a liberating hermeneutic must pass by the way of suspicion to retrieval. Suspicion leads to ideology criticism. But ideology criticism is then in the service of advocacy and reconstruction," 352.

29. See John Christopher Thomas, "Reading the Bible from within our Traditions: A Pentecostal Hermeneutic as Test Case," in *Between Two Horizons: Spanning New Testament Studies and Systematic Theology*, eds. Joel B. Green and Max Turner (Grand Rapids: Eerdmans, 2000) 120–22.

30. See chapter 2 for an explanation of the Pentecostal story.

central narrative convictions of Pentecostalism. The Pentecostal story must be interwoven into her personal story. This does not imply that one cannot be concerned about the larger Christian community or attempt to understand the Scripture from a different perspective or interpretive strategy, but it does mean that one's identity is shaped and formed by participating in a Pentecostal community.

In order for one to be a Pentecostal hermeneut (whether lay, clergy, educated or non-educated), one needs to be recognized as a Pentecostal. The hermeneut must share her story (testimony) and receive the important "amen" of affirmation from the community. Thus, one will need to have a clear and convincing testimony concerning his/her experiential relationship with the Lord Jesus Christ. The Full Gospel serves as the central narrative convictions of the Pentecostal community. The Full Gospel or Fivefold Gospel is a relational doxological articulation of the redemptive work of Jesus. Jesus is Savior, Sanctifier, Spirit Baptizer, Healer and Soon Coming King. This does not mean a Pentecostal hermeneut must have experienced every dimension of the Full Gospel, but she must be willing to participate in the Pentecostal story.[31] In this way, the theologian is an extension and participant of the community not an isolated individual reader.

The sharing of testimonies always involves and requires discernment from within the community. Therefore, one is not a Pentecostal hermeneut because one uses a Pentecostal method; there is no such thing as a Pentecostal method. Rather, one is a Pentecostal hermeneut because one is recognized as being a part of the community. The community, along with its concerns and needs, is the primary arena in which a Pentecostal hermeneut participates. The community actively, not passively, participates in the Pentecostal hermeneutic through discussion, testimony, and charismatic gifts.[32]

31. I am saying that the community requires the hermeneut to embrace the "Full Gospel" which encourages one to anticipate and participate in salvation, sanctification, healing, Spirit baptism while eagerly awaiting the soon return of Jesus. The point is that one has a particular relationship with Jesus and the community that is experiential and is defined by the "Full Gospel" message. The hermeneut is never alone in the interpretive process.

32. See Mark J. Cartledge, *Practical Theology: Charismatic and Empirical Perspectives* (Carlisle, UK: Paternoster, 2003) 52–60, for an important epistemological discussion concerning the function of testimony in Pentecostal and Charismatic communities.

Generally, academically trained biblical and theological hermeneuts will have an active leadership role in the Pentecostal community, whether it is as a pastor, teacher, or lay leader. One needs to appreciate that most Pentecostals who are a part of academic educational communities are credential-holding ministers of Pentecostal denominations.

The Pentecostal hermeneutic argues that the place to hear the present Word of God is the current context in which one lives. The past words of God (Scripture) then speak a present Word of God, which is to be believed and obeyed. The point of view of the reader/interpreter is not to be dismissed but embraced. This does not mean that Scripture cannot resist the reader's point of view. It does mean that the readers' community plays a significant role in what is found in Scripture and, then, what will become theologically normative for the community.

Pentecostals recognize that Scripture is the authoritative voice in the community and able to transform lives as it is inspired anew by the Holy Spirit. Pentecostals, like Christians in general, would want to hear the Scripture on its own terms, first and foremost. Yet, the hearing of Scripture is filtered through the Pentecostal narrative tradition. As a result of this, there is an interdependent dialogical and dialectical link between the community and the Scripture with the goal being communal and societal transformation.

Narrative Criticism: The Overarching Method

The readers (hermeneuts) in community select certain methods which they use in order to interpret texts. One of the important contributions of the hermeneut is the interpretive method. The method is not isolated from the person but becomes a tool that the hermeneut uses in the creative negotiation of theological meaning.

A narrative approach allows for the dialectic interaction of the text and reader in the negotiation of meaning. Pentecostals by their very nature are inherently storytellers. They primarily transmit their theology through oral means.[33] They have been conditioned to engage Scripture as story. The Bible is understood as a grand story—a metanarrative.[34] Thus,

33. W. J. Hollenweger, "The Pentecostal Elites and the Pentecostal Poor: A Missed Dialogue?" in *Charismatic Christianity as a Global Culture*, ed. Karla Poewe (Columbia: University of South Carolina Press, 1994) 201.

34. By metanarrative, I am referring to a grand story by which human societies and their individual members live and organize their lives in meaningful ways. The Christian

a narrative theological approach with a bent towards reader response would enable the Pentecostal community not only to critically interpret Scripture, but also to let Scripture critically interpret them.

Narrative Criticism's concern is similar to the Semiotic concern to keep a dialectic link between the reader and the text. This dialectic link between the narrative text and the reader insists on the reader responding to the text in ways that are signaled by the text for the production of meaning. Therefore, the empirical contemporary reader in community is an active participant in the production of meaning. The meaning(s) of the text is not simply found in the text, nor is it simply found in the reader but comes into existence in the *dialectic interaction* of the reader *with* the text.[35]

This dialectic interpretive tension is not simply a linear move of meaning from text to reader, as if in the classical literary interpretive sense that meaning is inherently and entirely found *in* the text, nor is the reader given freedom to construe meaning in the way that meets her creative concerns, which from that perspective allows the reader to stand *over* and *against* the text.[36] Once again, meaning is produced through the on-going interdependent dialectical interaction of the text and reader, both of which are necessary for a creative negotiation of meaning. Hence, neither the reader nor the text is to dominate the negotiation of meaning. The reader and text must work together in actualizing the potential meaning(s) of the text through the process of reading.[37] The reader in

metanarrative refers to the general Christian story about the meaning of the world and the God who created it and humanity's place in it. The Christian metanarrative is primarily dependent on the Bible for this general narrative. For a basic outline of the "Storyline" of the Christian metanarrative, see Gabriel Fackre, *The Christian Story: A Narrative of Basic Christian Doctrine*, 3rd ed. Vol. 1 (Grand Rapids: Eerdmans, 1996). Fackre writes that "Creation, Fall, Covenant, Jesus Christ, Church, Salvation, Consummation, . . . are acts in the Christian drama" with the understanding "That there is a God who creates, reconciles, and redeems the word" as "the 'Storyline,'" 8–9. See also Graig G. Bartholomew and Michael W. Goheen, *The Drama of Scripture: Finding Our Place in the Biblical Story* (Grand Rapids: Baker Academic, 2004).

35. Mark Allen Powell, *What is Narrative Criticism?* (Minneapolis: Fortress, 1990) 17–18.

36. Powell, *What is Narrative Criticism?* 16–21. Powell places Reader Response Criticism into three categories: the reader *over* the text, the reader *with* the text and, the reader *in* the text. He argues that Narrative Criticism falls into the third category, hence a more "objective" interpretive theory. I am arguing that there is much more overlap between Reader Response and Narrative Criticism.

37. Wolfgang Iser, *The Act of Reading: A Theory of Aesthetic-Response* (London: Routledge, 1978) 34–35.

community and the text make different kinds of contributions to the production of meaning, which allows the communicative event to succeed. This interdependent dialectical and dialogical interactive process is reinforced by Narrative Criticism's concern to follow the unfolding plot and its interaction with characters, settings, and events in the story world of the narrative. This also allows for Narrative Criticism to spill over into Reader Response Criticism.[38]

In sum, Narrative Criticism offers a text centered interpretive approach that allows for the socio-cultural context in which the text was generated to inform the contemporary reader, but in no way does it allow for it to dominate or control the interpretation of the text. Instead, the text is appreciated for what it is–a narrative; thus, the interpreter is concerned with the poetic features and structure of the story as a world in itself. The text invites the reader to negotiate meaning through a dialectical process of reading. Narrative critics are concerned to follow the responsive clues of the narrative from the perspective of its implied reader. Yet, the implied reader (whether a hypothetical construct of the text or a hypothetical construct in the mind of the empirical reader) necessitates the involvement of the empirical reader in the production of meaning. This affirms the importance of Reader Response Criticism. A Narrative-Reader Response approach would allow the text to give formative guidance without determining the actual response of the readers.

The imagination of the real reader shaped in community is vital to the reader's ability to comprehend the text. In this way, a Pentecostal would read the Bible as she would any other text or experience, namely, through the utilization of her imagination[39] shaped and formed in the

---

38. Stephen D. Moore, *Literary Criticism and the Gospels: The Theoretical Challenge* (New Haven, CT: Yale University Press, 1989) 73. Moore correctly points out that Reader Response Criticism is not "a conceptually unified criticism; rather it is a spectrum of contrasting and conflicting positions," 72. Also Powell, *What is Narrative Criticism?* 21, who writes, "narrative criticism and dialectic modes ('with the text') of reader response are most similar and they may eventually become indistinguishable."

39. I recognize that the Bible contains many forms of genre with narrative being the most prevalent. However, a few Bible critics recognize the value of narrative, as it is a necessary backdrop to the non-narrative portions of Scripture. See for example Norman R. Petersen, *Rediscovering Paul: Philemon and the Sociology of Paul's Narrative World* (Philadelphia: Fortress, 1985) and Ben Witherington III, *Paul's Narrative Thought World: The Tapestry of Tragedy and Triumph* (Louisville: Westminster/John Knox, 1994). Narrative as a theological overarching category of all Scripture necessitates one to locate a passage of a biblical text into the Scripture's dramatic story.

Pentecostal community by means of its narrative tradition and with her ears open to the Spirit.

The community, along with Scripture's potential polyvarient understandings, becomes the necessary participant in the ongoing interpretive process. The community engages the biblical text and so produces meaningful readings in ways that attempt to maintain the interdependent interactive dialogical relationship between the text and the community. The community, not an isolated reader, will negotiate the meaning through discussion and discernment as a direct address to the community. In doing so, the community will remain more faithful to the interpretive process of the first century Christian community then the isolated individual of the Modern age.[40] As Richard Hays demonstrates through examining the Apostle Paul's writings,

> Our account of Paul's interpretive activity has discovered no systematic exegetical procedures at work in his reading of Scripture. . . . his [Paul's] comments characteristically emphasize the immediacy of the text's word to the community rather than providing specific rules of reading. . . . Paul reads the text as bearing direct reference to his own circumstances . . . [and] that Scripture is rightly read as a word of address to the [present] eschatological community of God's people.[41]

In short, this Pentecostal hermeneutical strategy will embrace a narrative critical methodology while simultaneously affirming the Pentecostal community as the arena for the making of meaning. Interpretation is the result of a creative negotiation of meaning, and this meaning is always done from the particular context of an actual "reader in community." Croatto argues that the Bible is a present living word for the believing community. "As a result, what is genuinely relevant is not the 'behind' of a text, but its 'ahead,' its 'forward'—what it suggests as a pertinent message for the life of the one who seeks it out."[42] Hence, it is the reading of the Scripture from a

40. See Richard B. Hays, *Echoes of Scripture in the Letters of Paul* (New Haven, CT: Yale University Press, 1989) 161, 183–85. Hays argues that "if we learned from Paul how to read Scripture, we would read it primarily as a narrative of promise and election . . . ecclesiocentrically . . . in the service of proclamation . . . as participants in the eschatological drama of redemption." Pentecostal communities read the Scripture "as the people of the end time," from a narrative perspective of promise and from within the community as a word for the present which requires the interaction of the Holy Spirit.

41. *Echoes of Scripture*, 160, 166. See also McGrath, *Genesis of Doctrine*, 56.

42. Croatto, *Biblical Hermeneutics*, 50ff.

new praxis and in community that opens up valid yet multiple meanings of biblical texts.[43] Therefore, a Pentecostal reading would not only pay attention to the poetic features and the structure of the text, but would also fully affirm the importance of the contemporary Christian community's participation in the making of meaning. The Pentecostal model would desire to keep the making of meaning in creative interdependent dialectic tension between the text and the community, which is always moving into new and different contexts. In this manner, the making of meaning is a constructive ongoing cooperation between the text and community of faith. The Pentecostal community's theological conviction that the word of God speaks to the present eschatological community collapses the distance between the past and present allowing for creative freedom in the community's acts of interpretation.

The primary constraint that contemporary Pentecostals employ in order to limit their interpretive freedom is their tradition. This constraint is theological more so than methodological. Pentecostals would shout a hearty, "amen" to Hays's argument that all of Scripture must be interpreted in light of and as a witness to the Gospel of Jesus. "Scripture must be read as a witness to the Gospel of Jesus Christ. No reading of Scripture can be legitimate if it fails to acknowledge the death and resurrection of Jesus as the climatic manifestation of God's righteousness."[44] Therefore, a theological constraint provided by the reading of sacred Scripture as God's story with an emphasis upon the Gospel of Jesus Christ provides stability for the community in the making of meaning.

THE CONTRIBUTION OF THE HOLY SPIRIT

The theological interpretive strategy which I am proposing is a tridactic negotiation for meaning. I have described the contributions of the biblical text and community. Now I will address the contributions of the Holy Spirit to the hermeneutical process.

Explaining the contribution of the Holy Spirit is more difficult due to the realization that the Holy Spirit, although affirmed as being a present and active personal participant in the interpretive process, is nonetheless dependent upon the community's sensitivity and Scripture's perspicuity. The Holy Spirit's voice is heard in and through the individuals in commu-

43. For Croatto the new context of praxis is the fight against oppression.
44. See Hays, *Echoes of Scripture*, 191.

nity as well as in and through Scripture (which may be words of correction, reproof, or even a word of resistance to a certain biblical statement).[45] The Spirit's voice is not reduced to or simply equated with the biblical text or the community, but is connected to an interdependent upon these as a necessary means for expressing the past-present-future concerns of the Social Trinity. The Holy Spirit has more to say than Scripture, yet it will be scripturally based. The community must read and discern the signs and the sounds of the Spirit amongst the community in dialogical relationship with the Scriptures.

The role of the Holy Spirit in the hermeneutical process is to lead and guide the community in understanding the present meaningfulness of Scripture as the community theologically understands its relationship with the Social Trinity.[46] This ministry of the Holy Spirit is an extension of the ministry of the incarnate, crucified, ascended, and glorified Christ.[47] Therefore human societies in general and the Christian community in particular have not been abandoned by the living presence of God as a result of the ascension of Christ Jesus. The Holy Spirit, believed to be a real personal participant in the life of the Christian, enables the Christian in community to live faithfully with the living God as the community continues the mission of Jesus in the world.[48] Hence the Spirit does speak and has more to say than just Scripture.[49] This requires the community to discern the Spirit in the process of negotiating the meaning of the bibli-

45. For example, Pentecostals who affirm women in pastoral leadership look to other Scriptures as they resist certain texts of terror—specifically 2 Tim 2:11–12. Women who feel called to be in leadership "testify" that the Spirit has called them and cite certain Scriptures to support this claim. My point is that Scripture does not call people into leadership ministry but the Spirit does and the Spirit uses Scripture and community in the process.

46. I agree with Trevor Hart's statement in his "Tradition, Authority, and a Christian Approach to the Bible as Scripture" in *Between Two Horizons*, 203, that the Holy Spirit is not simply "an aid at getting at the meaning of Scripture" but instead "the Spirit is God's relatedness to us in the event of meaning through which he addresses us."

47. See the Gospel of John chapters 13–17, in Jesus's farewell discourse, he speaks of the importance of the Holy Spirit's ministry to the Christian community and human society.

48. Fowl, *Engaging Scripture*, 99.

49. See Rickie D. Moore, "A Letter to Frank Macchia," and Frank D. Macchia, "A Reply to Rickie Moore," *Journal of Pentecostal Theology* 17 (2000) 12–19, and James K. A. Smith, "The Closing of the Book: Pentecostals, Evangelicals and Sacred Writings," *Journal of Pentecostal Theology* 11 (1997) 49–71.

cal texts as the community faithfully carries on the mission of Jesus into new, different, and future contexts. "The Spirit's intervention and interpretive work is crucial if the followers of Jesus are faithfully to carry on the mission Jesus gives them."[50] For this reason, the voice of the Spirit cannot be reduced to simple recitation of Scripture; nonetheless, it will be connected to and concerned with Scripture because Scripture is God's story for all creation—especially humanity. Furthermore, this implies that previous theological understandings (in the form of official ecclesiastical doctrines) may need to be revised in the ongoing light revealed by the Spirit to the ecclesiastical community(s).

THE SPIRIT'S VOICE HEARD IN AND THROUGH A PENTECOSTAL COMMUNITY

Pentecostals desire the Holy Spirit to speak, lead and empower them in fulfilling the missionary task Jesus mandated to his followers. Pentecostals seek the Spirit's guidance in understanding Scripture and life experience in order to live obediently with God. The Spirit's voice is most actively discerned through the various gifts manifested in the community.

The Spirit's Voice in the Community

The worshipping community provides the primary context in which the Spirit's manifestation takes place. Personal testimonies, charismatic gifts, preaching, teaching, witnessing, serving the poor and praying are all acts of ministry that provide opportunities for the tangible manifestation of the Holy Spirit. The community is involved in discerning the authenticity of these manifestations and activities. The activities of the Pentecostal community's participants are "assessed and accepted or rejected."[51] Many times a belief and/or activity will be tolerated until more witnesses from the Spirit by means of Scripture and/or personal testimony can be given. The community provides the context for the manifestation/voice of the Spirit to be seen/heard and discerned.

Pentecostals will invite the Holy Spirit to manifest in various ways in the community. The purpose of these manifestations and community activities is to empower, guide, and transform the individuals in community so that the Pentecostal community can faithfully follow the Lord Jesus

---

50. Fowl, *Engaging Scripture*, 98.

51. Thomas, "Reading the Bible from within our Traditions," 119.

Christ. This requires the community to discern the Holy Spirit in the midst of the community's activities and manifestations and follow the Spirit's guidance. The individual's claim of being led by or speaking on behalf of the Spirit will be weighed in light of Scripture, the community's theological convictions and other individual testimonies. Thus, the community must interpret the manifestations of the Spirit.[52] "Experience of the Spirit shapes the reading of Scripture, but Scripture most often provides the lens through which the Spirit's work is perceived and acted upon."[53] The Christian community provides the dynamic context in which the Spirit is actively invited to participate in the theological negotiation of meaning.

DISCERNING THE SPIRIT'S VOICE COMING FROM OUTSIDE THE COMMUNITY

The Pentecostal story has placed missionary outreach as the very heartbeat of God's dramatic story and thus the primary purpose of the Pentecostal community's existence.[54] Pentecostals have and continue to embrace with great vigor the missionary task of reaching all people with the Gospel. They proclaim the Full Gospel to all who will listen in prayerful hope that non-Christians will respond to God's gracious salvific invitation to embrace Jesus and join the Pentecostal community. This passion for missional activity has encouraged Pentecostals to take the Gospel to the ends of the earth and thereby spreading the Full Gospel into regions outside of their cultural context and geographical locations. Pentecostals, especially those discerned to simultaneously have a missionary call and a local layperson call, evangelistically engage and confront other individuals in the community. Pentecostals do not stand from a distance; they get involved with other people while retaining their allegiance to their Pentecostal community. The engagement with other communal stories allows for

52. Fowl, *Engaging Scripture*, correctly points out that "it is important to recognize that the presence of miraculous signs is not a straightforward event," 104. The community must discern if the miraculous sign is of the Holy Spirit and what the sign is signifying to the community.

53. Fowl, *Engaging Scripture*, 114. This writer agrees with Fowl who argues that it is impossible in practice "to separate and determine clearly whether a community's scriptural interpretation is prior to or dependent upon a community's experience of the Spirit," 114.

54. See Steven J. Land, *Pentecostal Spirituality: A Passion for the Kingdom* (Sheffield, UK: Sheffield Academic Press, 1993).

openness to the voice of the Spirit to come to them from outside the Pentecostal community.

Pentecostals will not limit the work of the Spirit to their community, but will recognize that God's prevenient grace has been bestowed upon all of humanity. Furthermore, they fully expect the Holy Spirit to be actively working upon and speaking into the lives of all people, Christians and non-Christians. This underscores the importance of the Holy Spirit being active upon people before the Pentecostal missionaries arrive. Pentecostals, through their hospitable missionary outreach, have developed relationships with people outside their community and have discerned the presence of the Spirit in these foreign communities.[55] As a result, the Pentecostals will discern what the Spirit is saying to them from outside their community, which may be both typical and, yet, surprising for the Pentecostal community. In this way, the Spirit may speak from outside the Pentecostal community by means of speaking through Pentecostal missionaries, evangelists, recent converts, and those of us who engage in theological discussions with others outside of our tradition. Once again the community, Scripture, and Spirit are all necessary participants in the making of theological meaning with the community energized by the Spirit being the arena in which the Scripture and the Spirit converge.

THE SPIRIT'S VOICE COMES IN AND THROUGH THE SCRIPTURE

Generally, Pentecostals hold to a "high view" of Scripture. The Bible is understood to be an authoritative and trustworthy testimony about the Living God produced by humans that were inspired by the Holy Spirit. Scripture is affirmed as the sacred narrative of the Living God's revelation to humanity and specifically to the covenant community. Because of this belief, "Pentecostals regard the Scripture as normative and seek to live their lives in light of its teaching."[56] Pentecostals read Scripture for more than just information; they read with a desire to relationally know the living God and do the will of God. Reading Scripture, then, is a means of grace for experiencing redemptive transformation. Therefore, Pentecostals,

---

55. This would include officially recognized missionaries and local communities made up of both laity and clergy. Every Pentecostal is to be a witness for Jesus Christ.

56. Thomas, "Reading the Bible from within Our Traditions," 110.

both laity and academicians, actively invite the Holy Spirit to inspire the community and reveal meaningful understanding of Scripture.

How does the Spirit speak in and through the Scripture? The community must discern the Holy Spirit's voice, and the Holy Spirit must be granted an opportunity to be actively involved in the hermeneutical process. As Thomas argues, the Holy Spirit's involvement in the interpretive process as narrated in Acts 15, "heavily influenced the choice and use of Scripture" in resolving the thorny issues concerning the Gentiles' inclusion into the early Jewish Christian community.[57] This indicates that the Holy Spirit's presence was not passive but active in guiding and directing the community's engagement with Scripture. The participants in the Jerusalem Council could offer much Scriptural support concerning God's rejection of Gentiles, but not all of the Old Testament supports such a notion. Hence, when Scripture (both Old and New Testaments) offer diverse and even contradictory information concerning a particular practice or concern, the Spirit can direct the congregation through experience, visions, gifts, and testimonies towards a new theological understanding. This new understanding is rooted in Scripture, yet, moves beyond it. The community, then, must discern the Holy Spirit's involvement in the present context of the Christian community.

Pentecostals affirm that the primary context for the interpretation of Scripture is the believing community. Scripture as a grand metanarrative is celebrated as a gift of God's grace to the community. Personal faith in Jesus Christ as messiah is affirmed as a necessary aspect of the entire interpretative process. The interpretive concern of the community is to come to an understanding of what the Spirit is saying to the community in and through the biblical text(s). The Spirit has more to say than Scripture, but it is understood to be scripturally sound. Furthermore, the reading of Scripture (both personal and communal) offers a sacramental opportunity for the Spirit to work redemptively in the life of the readers.[58]

57. Ibid., 118.

58. See M. Robert Mulholland Jr., *Shaped by The Word: The Power of Scripture in Spiritual Formation*, rev. ed. (Nashville: Upper Room, 2000).

CONCLUSION

The Pentecostal theological hermeneutic being advocated encourages a tridactic dialectical and dialogical interdependent relationship between Scripture, Spirit, and Community. The Holy Spirit is the most significant person in the conversation. The model finds biblical support in Acts 15 and is a hermeneutical strategy that is a product of the Pentecostal identity. The particular method will be a Narrative-Reader Response approach from a semiotic understanding of language. The method, however, is not as important as the conversation that transpires among the community as it engages the Scripture and as it discerns the Spirit. The theological hermeneutic will be practiced by Pentecostal hermeneuts in community seeking the creative guidance and input of the Holy Spirit. The readers in community, the text, and the Holy Spirit are conversational participants in the tridactic negotiation for theological meaning. Therefore, this is a pneumatically grounded ecclesiastical community that opens itself up to other communities (both Christian and non-Christian) who are willing to dialogue with us as we seek to hear what the Spirit is saying.

7

Liberating Hermeneutics

The Intersections of Pentecostal Mission
and Latin American Theology in the Margins [1]

LATIN AMERICAN LIBERATION THEOLOGY
AND HERMENEUTICS

WE ARE CONCERNED THAT many Pentecostal traditions and churches in the USA, especially those who have lost connection to those living in the margins of society, are losing their *early* holistic missional practices. The ministry of early Pentecostals, even though most were not directly engaging in social action for changes in state legislation, brought transformation to the poor and destitute as well has hope to the lower income working classes. Currently, in other places outside of the USA, we see clear examples of Pentecostal communities' proclaiming the Full Gospel without separating the spiritual from the social or using social ministry as a means to spiritual ministry. These Pentecostal communities continue to practice the Full Gospel holistically, as did many of the early Pentecostals. We believe these communities can offer important, critical hermeneutical and theological insights for many contemporary Pentecostals living in the West. The marginal Pentecostal communities' hermeneutical practices and perspectives resonate with early Pentecostalism's understanding of

1. This chapter was jointly authored by Kenneth J. Archer and Richard E. Waldrop. Waldrop was Associate Professor of World Mission and Evangelism at the Church of God Theological Seminary and is Missionary Educator with Church of God World Missions, both in Cleveland, TN. A version of this paper was presented as a luncheon conversation with Jürgen Moltmann at the Society for Pentecostal Studies and Wesleyan Theological Society Third Joint Meeting, Durham, North Carolina, March 13–15, 2008.

the mission of God. The vitality of Pentecostalism is its robust spirituality of transformation for those in the margins.

In this chapter we will place Latin American liberation hermeneutics in dialogue with early North American Pentecostalism and current Latin American Pentecostal Liberation theology in order to demonstrate that there are significant commonalties. The concern is to revision a contemporary missional theology for certain North American Pentecostal churches that is in keeping with early Pentecostal practices. Furthermore, the missional theology proposed is informed by Pentecostal communities who are living in the margins and transforming their communities.

A Hermeneutic of Suspicion and Retrieval

In a general sense, all Liberation theologies employ some aspect of a Liberationist hermeneutic.[2] The Liberationist hermeneut attempts to demonstrate how the framework of interpretation of the dominant culture continues to suppress those on the margins. In this way, a "hermeneutic of suspicion" seeks "to penetrate beneath their surface-function *to expose their role as instruments of power, domination and or social manipulation.*"[3] Liberationists all utilize a "hermeneutic of suspicion." Often, Nietzsche, Marx, and Freuds's works are adapted critically in order to analyze the narrative of society's powerful.[4] Identifying the power structures is only a

2. Anthony Thiselton, *New Horizons in Hermeneutics* (Grand Rapids: Eerdmans; Paternoster, 1980) 410. Thiselton observes that the Liberationists share three common traits. He writes: "First and foremost, they construct critiques of the *frameworks of interpretation* which are used or presupposed in dominant traditions. . . . These frameworks transmit pre-understandings and symbolic systems which perpetuate, it is argued, the ideologies of dominate traditions. Second, liberation, black, and feminist approaches offer alternative *re-interpretations of biblical texts from the standpoint of a particular context of experience and action*. . . . Third, each approach seeks *critical* tools and resources to unmask those uses of biblical texts *which serve the social interests of domination, manipulation, or oppression*, to expose them as what they are. Each claims to embody some *critical* principle, by means of which to reveal the unjust goals and bases of manipulative interpretive devices and procedures" (his italics). I would add that the "principle" cannot be understood as right theory leading to right practice but must be appreciated as praxis—action and reflection leading to further action connected to living within community.

3. Thiselton, *New Horizons*, 379.

4. Ibid. 46–47. See Leonardo Boff and Clodovis Boff, *Introducing Liberation Theology* (Turnbridge Wells, UK: Barns & Oats, 1987) 27–28. Boff writes that "liberation theology uses Marxism purely as an *instrument*. . . . liberation theology freely borrows from Marxism certain 'methodological pointers' that have proved fruitful in understanding the

partial task of a Liberationist hermeneutic. Liberation theologians must provide an alternative, yet appropriate, reading of Scripture. Because Scripture serves a primary means for Christian liberation, they will also employ a "hermeneutic of retrieval."

Liberation hermeneutics seek to unmask uses of biblical passages which serve the interests of the dominating power or cultural structures. The concern is to reveal the *inappropriate* ways Scriptures are woven into the predominant ideological narrative of a society—a difficult and risky task when the contemporary society at large understands itself to be a "Christian nation."[5] Those who draw upon the Scriptures to support an inappropriate narrative are consciously and unconsciously appealing to God to substantiate such coercive narratives. Furthermore, Liberation theologians recognize that all interpretive readings are culturally dependent and inherently contain socio-ideological perspectives. This would be true of their interpretive readings, which they acknowledge. The interpretive method, practices, and readings are ideologically biased. Hermeneutical strategies reflect the biases of those using them. They challenge the so-called neutral-scientific reading of Scripture and offer it as further evidence of a manipulative ploy of the powerful.

A Christian Liberationist theologian's goal is to present alternative readings of Scripture through the use of a critical hermeneutic in order to bring liberation to those on the margins.[6] The Liberation hermeneutic of suspicion and retrieval's ultimate concern is "to integrate biblical interpretation into an agenda of personal conversion and social transformation."[7]

Latin American Liberation theologians begin from their concrete experience of the oppression of the poor. They utilize some critical strat-

---

world of the oppressed, such as: the importance of economic factors; attention to class struggle; the mystifying power of ideologies, including religious ones" (their italics) 28.

5. Some Liberationists, especially but not exclusively Feminists will deconstruct both the horizon of the text, the text, and the contemporary horizon of the readers. For example, See Elisabeth Schüssler Fiorenza, *In Memory of Her: A Feminist Theological Reconstruction of Christian Origins*, 10th anniv. ed. (New York: Crossroad, 1994) xii–xlii, "Introduction to the Tenth Anniversary Edition: Remember the Struggle" for a succinct summary of Fiorenza's feminist epistemology and interpretive practice.

6. The interpretive "exegetical" method(s) are typical and generally accepted ways of interpreting Scripture, yet through the experience of the oppressed.

7. Sandra M. Schneiders, "Feminist Hermeneutics," in *Hearing The New Testament: Strategies for Interpretation*, ed. Joel Green (Grand Rapids: Eerdmans, 1995) 349.

egy in the rereading of Scripture in order to retrieve from the Scripture liberation for the oppressed. However, like all liberation readings they begin with the present experience of oppression. Leonardo and Clodovis Boff write:

> The Liberation theologian goes to the scriptures bearing the whole weight of the problems, sorrows and hopes of the poor, seeking light and inspiration from the divine word. This is a new way of reading the Bible: The hermeneutics of liberation.[8]

The Latin American Liberation theologian begins with the experience of unjust poverty. The clear emphasis upon the poor results from a thorough understanding of the socio-economic situation of the poor in Latin America. It is not enough to be sympathetic from a safe distance. One must live among the poor in order to have true "com-passion." The person utilizing a Liberationist hermeneutic must experience the poverty, the humiliation and economic deprivation of the poor. Solidarity with the poor is coming along side by entering into the lived experience of unjust poverty. Only after a substantial period of experiencing this poverty can one then begin to do theology as a Liberation theologian.[9] From this lived experience emerges a continuous dialogue between old ways of understanding and new ways of living. Liberation Theology draws upon the spirituality of the poor's transformative encounter with the Lord Jesus. The desire to imitate the historic Jesus in their present reality creates possibilities for personal and social transformation.[10] The ability to imitate the historic Jesus in the present context is through living in the Spirit. "Liberation is an all embracing process that leaves no dimension of human life untouched, because, when it is said and done, it expresses the saving action of God in history."[11]

8. Boff, *Introducing Liberation Theology*, 32.

9. Ibid., 3–5, 22–24. See also, Gustavo Gutiérrez, *A Theology of Liberation: History, Politics, and Salvation*, rev. ed. (Maryknoll, NY: Orbis, 1988), for his definition of the poor, xxi–xxii.

10. See especially Gutiérrez, *Theology of Liberation*, "Liberation and Salvation," 83–105.

11. Gustavo Gutiérrez, *We Drink from Our Own Wells: The Spiritual Journey of a People* (Maryknoll, NY: Orbis, 1984, 1994) 2.

A Theological Hermeneutic of Pastoral Praxis

Gutiérrez writes, "Theology does not produce pastoral activity; rather it reflects upon it. Theology must be able to find in pastoral activity the presence of the Spirit inspiring the action of the Christian community."[12] Theology is a secondary reflection upon the spirituality of the Christian community's journey with God. Latin American Liberation exegesis is closely connected to the pastoral practice of ministry in an ecclesial base community. The community, often led by informed priests or laity, searches the Scripture in order to find meaning for their present situation.[13] The community must participate in the responsibility of bringing about both personal and communal liberation. The Scripture plays a primary role by offering guidance, inspiration and transformative moments for the community's participation in God's salvific mission of liberation within human history.[14]

As is often pointed out, Liberation readings do not follow the same distancing approach as the historical critical methods, or even the more North American "evangelical" appropriation of historical-critical, exegetical methods. Instead of looking for the authorial intent of a passage in its past historical context with all the specialization of the academy, the pastoral leader as one in the community looks for textual meaning relevant to present life situations of the readers. The communitarian reading finds points of comparison between their experience and the experiences of

12. Gustavo Gutiérrez, *Theology of Liberation*, 9.

13. For one Liberation theologian's presentation of the role of the Base Communities participation biblical interpretation, see Carlos Mesters, "The Use of the Bible in Christian Communities of the Common People" in *The Bible and Liberation: Political and Social Hermeneutics*, eds. Norman K. Gottwald and Richard A. Horsley (Maryknoll, NY: Orbis, 1993) 3–16. For an important introduction with English translation of actual exegetical practice and readings of Base Communities see Christopher Rowland and Mark Corner, *Liberating Exegesis: The Challenges of Liberation Theology to Biblical Studies* (Louisville: Westminster John Knox, 1998). Concerning the vitality and necessity of the base communities for liberation, see Guillermo Cook, *The Expectation of the Poor: Latin American Basic Ecclesial Communities in Protestant Perspective* (Maryknoll, NY: Orbis, 1985).

14. For an expansion upon this important dimension of liberation from a Pentecostal perspective, see Ricardo E. Waldrop, "Misión Trinitaria e Historia Salvífica: Una Perspective Pentecostal," a paper presented at the Simposio Internacional Jürgen Moltmann, at the Universidad Evangélica Nicaragüense, Managua, Nicargua, October 2006 and forthcoming in English as "Trinitarian Mission and Salvation History: A Pentecostal Perspective" in *Passover, Pentecost and Parousia: Studies in Celebration of the Life and Ministry of R. Hollis Gause*, eds. S. J. Land, R. D. Moore, and J. C. Thomas (Blandford Forum: Deo, 2010).

characters of Scripture, in particular those who are marginalized. Most often the focus is on the Prophets and Gospels, with special attention given to the Lukan narrative as a continuation of the themes of exodus and liberation.[15] The goal is to hear the Word of God as being consistent with the past word of God centered upon the historic Jesus. The close reading of Scripture in the ecclesial base community is a practice that desires to be in continuity with early Christianity and at the same time recognizes the reader's present social and economic context as an important contribution in the production of textual meaning.[16] The reading/hearing of Scripture is the primary means to interpret life, because Scripture is not an object or artifact in need of being interpreted.[17] Gutiérrez writes, "We approach the Bible from our experience as believers and members of the church. It is in light of that experience that we ask our questions." "We indeed read the Bible, but we can also say that the Bible 'reads us.'" This practice often leads those asking questions to reformulate the questions in light of the Gospel.[18]

With similar pastoral concerns, Boff writes:

> Liberation hermeneutics reads the Bible as a book of life, not as a book of strange stories. The textual meaning is indeed sought, but only as a function of *practical* meaning: the important thing is not so much interpreting the text of scripture as interpreting life "according to the scriptures." Ultimately, this old/new reading aims to find contemporary actualization (practicality) for textual meaning.[19]

The goal of interpretation is holistic transformative action because textual meaning can only be understood in and through contemporary actualization. The Liberationist reading views the Bible as a semiotic language and the contemporary actualization as the new speech-act. The context in which to hear Scripture is not the past historical-cultural setting in which

---

15. The theme of the Exodus in liberation has been developed by Jorge Pixley. See his *Exodus* (New York: Abingdon, 2004), in the Global Bible Commentary series.

16. For a concise explanation of a praxis methodological approach to the interpretation of Scripture, see J. Severino Croatto, *Biblical Hermeneutics: Toward a Theory of Reading as the Production of Meaning* (Maryknoll, NY: Orbis, 1987).

17. See, Christopher Rowland and Mark Corner, *Liberating Exegesis*, chapter 2, "Foundation and Form of Liberation Hermeneutics," 35–84.

18. Gustavo Gutiérrez, *We Drink from Our Own Wells*, 34.

19. Boff, *Introducing Liberation Theology*, 34.

Scriptures were generated but in the present context of oppression. It is in the present context that Scripture speaks as the liberating Word of God. The Liberationist hermeneutic "is a hermeneutic that favors *application* rather than explanation" from the present perspective of the poor.[20]

González points out that Hispanic readers of Scripture are "looking at the same landscape" (that is the Bible), but from the perspective of the marginalized. We are seeking "an interpretation *of the Bible*, and not simply our experiences whether good or bad." The perspective is one shaped by marginalization, suffering and poverty.[21] The poor see things that others ignore or simply cannot see.

The liberating re-reading encourages the poor to act in ways others find unacceptable, challenging, troubling, or even noble. But it also presents readings which have been ignored or even unnoticed by European and American males.[22] Yet, the liberation reading is an insider reading of the Bible, a Christian communal reading by the poor for personal-communal transformation and new possibilities for social transformation.[23]

The methodology of ecclesial base community Bible reading follows a threefold process of seeing, judging, and acting.[24] By seeing, one starts with their experience of oppression and poverty. By judging, one asks questions concerning their situation, coming to an understanding of the situation in which they exist. They connect their experience of oppression to the story of deliverance from oppression as found in the Bible. The oppressed, then, act upon the Word for the transformation of human dignity and the transformation of social structures supporting oppression. In this way, reading is praxis, action-reflection upon the present situation in light of the Word of the Lord.[25]

In sum,

20. Ibid., 33.

21. Justo L. González, *Santa Bíblia: The Bible through Hispanic Eyes* (Nashville: Abingdon, 1996) 11–30, esp. 18.

22. This may not be as an acute problem as it once was because of the influence of Liberation Theologies upon as well as from within the academy.

23. For Gutiérrez, new possibilities can come into existence only in present historic praxis oriented to the future hope. This is the already and not yet eschatological nature of salvation; See 11–12, 93–97.

24. The following is from Rowland and Corner, *Liberating Exegesis*, 38.

25. An appreciation of the hermeneutical circle is built into the practice, only the move is dialogical from present to the past via the text, and then a return to the present situation with a transformative reading of the text related to wholistic salvation.

The theology of liberation offers us not so much a new theme for reflection as a *new way* to do theology. Theology as critical reflection on historical praxis is a liberating theology, a theology of the liberating transformation of the history of humankind and also therefore that part of humankind—gathered into *ecclesia*—which openly confesses Christ. This is a theology which does not stop with reflecting on the world, but rather tries to be part of the process through which the world is transformed. It is a theology which is open—in the protest against trampled human dignity, in the struggle against the plunder of the vast majority of humankind, in liberating love, and in building of a new, just, and comradely society—to the gift of the Kingdom of God.[26]

A PENTECOSTAL LIBERATING HERMENEUTIC FOR MISSION

Elsewhere, we have suggested that a contemporary Pentecostal hermeneutic should speak in a liberating voice with a post-Christendom accent.[27] We based this upon the early spirituality of Pentecostals, their Bible reading method, their understanding of the *missio Dei* and our concern that contemporary Pentecostal theology must be shaped from the spirituality of those living in the margins.[28]

The early Pentecostal hermeneutical practice functioned as a means of liberation for those who were marginalized by modernistic culture and mainline Christianity. Pentecostals employed a hermeneutic of suspicion and retrieval. They were suspicious of all forms of Christianity that did not preach and, more importantly, live the Full Gospel. Thus, they were able to retrieve from Scripture stories that encouraged women to preach the Gospel, the wealthy to share their prosperity generously, believers to

26. Gutiérrez, *Theology of Liberation*, 12.

27. In relation to the historic paradigms of mission, as Pentecostals, we agree with Alan Krieder and others that it is better to understand it from three historic paradigms of pre-Christendom, Christendom and post-Christendom. See Alan Krieder, "Beyond Bosch: The Early church and The Christendom Shift," *International Bulletin of Missionary Research* 29:2 (2005) 59–68.

28. Kenneth J. Archer, "Pentecostal Hermeneutics: Retrospect and Prospect," *Journal of Pentecostal Theology* (1996) 81; Kenneth J. Archer, *A Pentecostal Hermeneutic: Spirit, Scripture and Community* (Cleveland, TN: CPT, 2009); Ricardo Waldrop, "La teología de la liberación: Un enfoque crítico" in *Pastoralia* 7:15; Richard E. Waldrop, *A Historical and Critical Analysis of the Full Gospel Church of God of Guatemala*, a diss. submitted to Fuller Theological Seminary School of World Mission, Pasadena, CA, 1993.

practice peacemaking (pacifist lifestyle), and the community to exist as an alternative ecclesial community within the larger society all in response to the Lukan narrative (Acts 2; Luke 4).

Early Pentecostals, following the trajectory of their Holiness and Wesleyan forebears, heard biblical stories that emphasized concern for the poor and needy. They were concerned to spread the good news of the Gospel which meant the Lord Jesus could deliver them from demonic influence, sickness and spiritual death. All who called upon the Lord could become faithful followers of Jesus. Hence they heeded the call to participate in the mission of God. This meant the liberation of humans from sin, sickness and Satan, thus creating a "haven for the masses."[29]

The biblical stories, especially those related to Jesus and the Acts of the Apostles reaffirmed their understanding of the Pentecostal story that God was pouring out his Spirit in these last days upon the marginalized (Luke 4, Acts 2). Spirit baptism was God's means of empowering anyone—especially the marginalized—to become full-fledged participants in God's Reign. Hence, the Pentecostal central narrative convictions of the Fivefold Gospel provided a potent means for bringing unity, dignity and liberation to God's people. Liberation, however, would have come as a result of being saved *from* Satan's kingdom and *out of* fallen society, thus becoming a voluntary contrast community.

Early Pentecostalism emerged from the margins of society and continues to spread in the Global South of the majority world.[30] The Pentecostal hermeneutical practice has certain similarities expressed

---

29. The language of "haven of the masses" is typical of the social deprivation theory, used in analyses characteristic of early Pentecostalism such as Christian Lalive d'Epinay, *The Haven of the Masses: A Study of the Pentecostal Movement Chile* (London: Lutterworth,1969) and Robert Mapes Anderson, *Vision of the Disinherited: The Making of American Pentecostalism* (Peabody, MA: Hendrickson, 1979). While these analyses demonstrate the social location of early Pentecostal adherents, they are partial in their understanding of the early Pentecostal ethos. Early Pentecostalism was a liberation movement of, by, and for the poor. See Francisco Cartaxo Rolim, "El pentecostalismo a partir del pobre," *Christianismo y Sociedad* (1988:95). The so-called "social strike" practiced by early and mid-20th century Pentecostals cannot be fully understood apart from the harsh realities of life, social ostracism and their genuine self-understanding as the peculiar people of God in mission in the last days. For a critique of social deprivation as it relates to Pentecostalism, see also Archer, *A Pentecostal Hermeneutic*.

30. See Philip Jenkins, *The Next Christendom: The coming of Global Christianity* (New York: Oxford University Press, 2002).

by Liberationists—especially Latin American Liberation theologians.[31] Liberation theologians' emphasis upon the poor and their ecclesiastical, hermeneutical practice of base community readings that move from the present concrete experiential context to the biblical text (the opposite direction of the traditional historical methods) are important practices that intersect with early Pentecostal interpretative practices.

While differences do indeed exist, there are important points of intersection between early radical Pentecostal theology and the more recent Latin American Liberation theology.[32] A contemporary Pentecostal missional hermeneutic must embrace the same starting position as the Liberationist—the present context of the community. Both share a basic understanding that Scripture is to be read and heard in an ecclesiastical context. The ecclesiastical context is the local base community. The interpretive process is a grass roots communal activity.[33] The Pentecostal hermeneut must be entrenched within a Pentecostal community and in tune with the concrete realities of suffering, poverty and marginalization. This incarnational approach of being the people of God in solidarity with the suffering of humanity creates com-passion.

This compassionate practice affirms the Liberationist posture of living among the people; but, in this case, it is a Pentecostal community in which the Spirit is discerned and the Scripture is heard in the present context and obeyed. Therefore, the experience of poverty will be a reality for most Pentecostals in the Global South. But, the means

---

31. The inherent liberating impulse of Pentecostalism has also been connected with Feminist and African-American liberation theology.

32. See Miroslav Volf, "Materiality of Salvation: An Investigation in the Soteriologies of Liberation and Pentecostal Theologies." *Journal of Ecumenical Studies* 26 (1989) 447–67. Volf argues that both traditions share a similar soteriology which he identifies as a "*materiality of salvation*" (his italics). He writes, "Salvation is not merely a spiritual reality touching only an individual person's inner being but also has to do with *bodily* human existence" with is essential, not marginal, to the understanding of both soteriologies, 448. We are concerned with hermeneutics and how it relates to the mission of God. Volf further states that "it would be a worthwhile endeavor to compare the hermeneutic of liberation theology and the hermeneutic of Pentecostal theology," 448 n. 4.

33. See Cheryl Bridges Johns, *Pentecostal Formation: A Pedagogy Among the Oppressed* (Sheffield, UK: Sheffield Academic Press, 1993). This important work draws upon her critical reflection of the significant work of Paulo Freire, a Roman Catholic Latin American pedagogue, who pioneered the liberationist methodology of *conscientizacao* among the illiterate and poor classes of the continent.

of liberation will not come primarily from any particular reading of social reality, whether capitalist or socialist. It will only come through the Spirit of Life in engaged Pentecostal witness for the spiritual and social transformation of the world.[34] As Eldin Villafañe demonstrates, Hispanic Pentecostal spirituality "seeks to extend its self-understanding as the community of the Spirit *in* the world and *for* the world, but not *of* the world."[35]

The Pentecostal community embraces certain practices found in the Acts-Gospels narrative in order to continue the ministry of Jesus through the empowerment of the Spirit which is related to the mission of God. Therefore, Pentecostal communities should not embrace violence or militarism as a means for social transformation. But, in keeping with the early pacifism of the movement, we should embrace New Testament Christianity as the means to creating alternative communities within the diverse socio-economic contexts in which she finds herself.[36] An engaged Pentecostal community will compassionately practice the politics of Jesus.[37]

Early Pentecostals embraced a pacifist lifestyle because they believed this was how Jesus lived his life and how he wanted his followers to live their lives. Violence was never an acceptable means to changing the world systems.[38] Like Liberationists, these early Pentecostals read Scripture from their concrete situations and Christological perspective with the expecta-

---

34. We especially appreciate Jürgen Moltmann theological contributions concerning God's creative and redemptive work through the Holy Spirit. See his *God in Creation: A New Theology of Creation and the Spirit of God* (New York: Abingdon, 1993).

35. *The Liberating Spirit: Toward an Hispanic American Pentecostal Social Ethic* (Grand Rapids: Eerdmans, 1993) 193.

36. Kenneth J. Archer and Andrew S. Hamilton, "Anabaptism-Pietism and Pentecostalism: Scandalous Partners in Protest," in *Scottish Journal of Theology* 63:2 (2010) 185–202.

37. See John H. Yoder, *The Politics of Jesus: Vicit Agnus Noster* (Grand Rapids: Eerdmans, 1971) which is now a classic on the understanding of the Gospel to be a call to live nonviolently. From a distinctively Pentecostal perspective, see Paul Alexander, *Peace, Power and Pentecost: Nonviolence, Nationalism and Militarism in American Pentecostalism* (Telford, OR: Cascadia, 2007), and "Spirit Empowered Peacemaking: Toward a Pentecostal Charismatic Peace Fellowship," *Journal of the European Pentecostal Theological Association* (2002) 22.

38. For additional Pentecostal resources on peacemaking, including quotations from early Pentecostal pioneers on the topic of pacifism, patriotism and militarism, see www.pcpj.org.

tion of hearing the Spirit. The Pentecostal Christological perspective was summarized through the Full Gospel, and they embraced nonviolence as a way of life.[39] Early Pentecostals thought they were apolitical and attempted to protest society by creating a Christian community within it. They saw themselves as a separate community living within a fallen society. Thus, a Pentecostal missional hermeneutic will always recognize that Christianity must not be confused with any national ideology or economic system. The Kingdom of God exists on earth within Christian communities and over against all human institutions, including the institutional church and civil religion. For this reason, the Reign of God should not be confused with any particular nation or any particular Christian tradition.

A contemporary Pentecostal missional theology will share the Liberationists concern for praxis. It is not enough to be orthodox in beliefs. The community must also be concerned with orthopraxy and orthopathy. These concerns are rooted in the Pentecostal narrative tradition. The Pentecostal community goes to the Scripture with an expectation to hear a divine word for her situation. Thus, there is openness to the Holy Spirit to speak in and through the sacred Scriptures in order to find guidance and character formation, so that the members of the community may participate rightly in the *missio Dei*. For Pentecostals, the very act of reading is a spiritual act of worship because the community reads Scripture in order to hear, encounter, and obey the Holy Spirit. Obedience is seen as an act of worship and witness.

In an effort to exemplify the kind of creative and progressive Pentecostal missional theology described in this paper, we will introduce briefly the pastoral praxis and theological reflection of Darío López Rodríguez, a Peruvian pastor and leading Latin American Pentecostal theologian.[40]

---

39. Boff, *Introducing Liberation Theology*. "We hardly need to say that any book of the Bible has to be read in a christological key that is based on the high point of revelation as found in the Gospels," 35. One wonders then how some liberationists and so many contemporary Euro-American Pentecostals can justify the use of violence, if the Gospels are to be the lens and key for reading the rest of the Bible.

40. See the following selection of works: *Los evangélicos y los derechos humanos: La experiencia social del Concilio Nacional Evangelico del Perú 1980–1992* (Lima: Puma, 1998), *Pentecostalismo y transformación social: Mas allá de los estereotipos, las críticas se enfrentan con los hechos* (Buenos Aires: Kairos, 2000), *El nuevo rostro del pentecostalismo latinoamericano* (Lima: Puma, 2002), *La fiesta del Espiritu: Espiritualidad y celebración pentecostal* (Lima: Puma, 2006), *Artesanos de la paz: Modelos bíblicos de reconciliación* (Lima: Puma, 2006).

López draws primarily upon his pastoral ministry in the marginal neighborhood of Villa María del Triúnfo, comprised largely of the working class poor on the outskirts of Lima, Perú. In his work, he uses the everyday struggles of his parishioners as points of departure for developing his approach to holistic mission. These include three interrelated classes of people who are treated as subjects and participants in the mission of God and not mere dispensable objects in the values of the neo-liberal economic system of the day. Children, women, and immigrants comprise the three classes.[41]

López's pastoral praxis moves him and his community to minister to neglected and vulnerable children of which over 200 receive education and nutrition on a daily basis. People in the local church give of their time and means in order to provide this ministry. It needs to be pointed out that the children are considered part of the local church community. López has stated many times that the most difficult theological questions that he is called upon to address come from the children. These questions serve as cues from which he is able to write and develop both local church curricula and his more sophisticated academic theological work.

Impoverished and abused women receive holistic ministry. As a result, many of these women have become actively involved in community service and social advocacy organizations, further ministering to children and others in wider society. These women have organized protest marches to the government palace to demand fair and compassionate treatment for needy children in Peruvian society resulting in actual changes made to the laws governing the treatment of minors.[42]

Many of the members of the local church, including Pastor López, come from the ranks of the immigrant population of the indigenous cultures of the Peruvian highlands. The indigenous people have suffered severely from the brutal attacks, in recent years, of the Shining Path guer-

41. Darío López Rodríguez, *The Liberating Mission of Jesus: the Message of the Gospel of Luke,* translated by Richard E. Waldrop and under review for publication. "Solidarity with the marginalized, more than an interesting theological discourse or relevant ideological proposal, has to be an everyday experience that rests upon the risks of publicly identifying oneself with those who are socially and culturally marginalized. Consequently, to sit at the same table and break bread in fellowship with the disinherited of this world forms part of a missionary lifestyle," 23.

42. See "De excluidas a protagonistas: Mujeres pentecostales y organizaciones populares," chapter 3 in *El nuevo rostro del pentecostalismo latinomericano.*

rilla movement and the Peruvian army. These displaced peasants and farmers have found a refuge and a place of service at the Mount Sinai Church of God.

After many years of pastoral ministry, López was able to further develop his theological vocation. He completed a PhD through the Oxford Centre for Mission Studies, where he wrote a thesis on the neglected topic of the Evangelical church and human rights in Peru. This was the first of many theological literary works which adroitly integrates the complex issues of church and society in a way reminiscent of other Liberationists' approach. As has been pointed out above, he begins with the concrete social and political realities in which his parishioners are immersed. From their reality, Scripture is searched and the Spirit is sought for the empowerment of holistic liberation in the mission of God. Their hermeneutical task is similar to the Liberationist methodology of action-reflection or better seeing, judging, and acting.[43] Yet, his community which is of, for, and by the poor have all the characteristic signs of a Pentecostal church. These include passionate anointed preaching, fervent communal prayer, expressive and lively worship, manifestations of the charismatic gifts, special prayer for the healing of the sick and broken hearted, encouragement for women in pastoral leadership and active evangelism in the community resulting in the establishment of daughter churches. For López, the rationale for such a missional community is the liberating mission of Christ Jesus as portrayed in the Gospels, and in particular, from a Lukan perspective (Luke 4). López demonstrates from the Lukan Gospel that,

> From the world of the poor, a holistic perspective of mission is woven which points toward the transformation of all things, to radical discipleship brought about by an unbreakable faith in the God of life, to the affirmation of the uncompromising value of hu-

43. See his *The Liberating Mission of Jesus: The Message of Gospel of Luke,* which was written as a Bible study book. This work is an attempt to explain the message of the third gospel and proposes that the liberating message of Jesus has two non-negotiable, main points: the universality of the mission and the special love of God for the poor and the excluded. The central thesis is an understanding of mission in terms of liberation as understood from a Lukan perspective of salvation which gives no place to the more modernistic dichotomy between the spiritual and the social or between the individual and community. López interacts with current Latin American theologians' writings, such as José Míguez Bonino, Guillermo Cook, Gustavo Gutierrez, René Padilla and leading Lukan scholars, such as Hans Conzelmann, Joel Green, Philip Esler, not to mention the older, traditional works and scholarly, evangelical, exegetical commentaries.

man life as a gift from God, to peacemaking and to the affirmation of the dignity of all human beings as creations of God.[44]

López emphasizes in his writings and in his lifestyle a holistic mission of salvation. He takes seriously both the so-called physical and spiritual dimensions of human existence. His practice of holistic mission rightly blurs modernity's preoccupation with inward religion and outward politics by subverting both to the relationality of God's liberating salvation. Unlike most conservative Evangelicals and Pentecostals, he does not reduce the Gospel to spiritual, inward salvation; and, unlike some doctrinaire Liberationists, he does not reduce the Gospel to economic and political salvation. Instead, these dimensions are held together in the liberating mission of the Spirit, in the Son, and on behalf of God's creation, especially humanity.

These themes run through López's many theological treatises which, although unknown to the English speaking world, have gained a substantial reading in Latin America. López's work represents the cutting edge of a new generation of progressive Latin American Pentecostals which would be instructive to the increasingly institutionalized Anglo-pentecostal churches of North America.

In Summary, we have identified points of commonality between Liberationist praxis and Pentecostal missional theology through the common lens of a liberating hermeneutic emerging out of the margins. The points of intersection were: the shared contextual reading of Scripture with the ecclesial community being the primary hermeneut, pastoral praxis with, by, and for the poor and marginalized sectors of society, the practice of holistic mission and the primacy of the Lukan narrative for the understanding of the mission.

44. López, *Liberating Mission of Jesus*, 28.

Concluding Remarks

YOU HAVE TRAVERSED THROUGH my theological journey. I am grateful to you, the readers, for your perseverance. I hope that you have found this to be a fruitful experience. This work is provisional and in process. The Spirit is still speaking, Scripture is still informing, and the testimonies of others are still being heard.

I do believe that Pentecostalism is a distinct living tradition. There are various forms of Pentecostalism, but these forms are vibrant performances of the spirituality of the Pentecostal community. To define Pentecostalism solely upon a so-called classical Pentecostal view is too narrow and misleading. It is misleading because many Charismatics would also affirm the Baptism in the Holy Spirit as an event subsequent to regeneration and initially evidenced by speaking in other tongues. They modify their theological tradition; however, they do not entirely renovate it. It is too narrow because the classical Pentecostal view does not take into consideration the significance of the overarching story which holds the tradition together. I am convinced that Pentecostalism is a renovation of already existing Christian traditions which bring forth a new living *Christian* tradition. Pentecostal spirituality-theology is articulated through the central narrative convictions, and, at the very core is the doxological confession of the Fivefold Gospel or variations of the Full Gospel.

Throughout these various essays I have attempted to allow the doxological confessions connected to the Fivefold Gospel to shape the theological presentation. Chapter five may seem to be an exception. However, chapter five is addressing the relational openness of God and a biblical synergistic view of soteriology. Pentecostal worship and witness implicitly and at times overtly communicates such understandings.

Pentecostalism embraces a synergistic soteriology. Forms of monergistic soteriology are simply incompatible with Pentecostal theology. I think one can be a Wesleyan Pentecostal. Yet, a Wesleyan who embraces a distinct experience of the Baptism in the Holy Spirit with some kind of outward physical evidence may prefer to be identified as a Charismatic Wesleyan. I am doubtful one can be a Reformed Pentecostal, in the more restrictive Protestant Scholastic and classical Calvinistic sense. I think it would be better to say that one can be a Charismatic and Reformed. Here I am simply trying to tease out the various differences without devaluing the Reformed tradition. Some important differences between the two traditions are the longstanding Reformed tradition's cessationist worldview, monergistic soteriology and desire to establish and maintain Christian commonwealths. From my perspective, Pentecostalism's understanding of soteriology has more in common with Eastern Orthodoxy and Roman Catholicism than Protestant Scholasticism which clearly resurfaces in North American Calvinistic Evangelicalism.

Pentecostal ecclesiology envisions the Church as a contrast community that extends the mission of Christ through the personal powerful presence of the Holy Spirit. Pentecostalism should avoid forms of ecclesiology that embrace Theonomy or other resurgent forms of Christian commonwealth. Pentecostal ecclesiology has more in common with the Anabaptists than the Magisterial Reformers. However, Pentecostal theology will engage in social concerns and social reforms. These are just a few observations which I hope illustrate the importance of appreciating Pentecostalism as a distinct Christian tradition.

I do not claim to speak for the entire Pentecostal community; I speak a local theology born out of my primary Christian community of Pentecostalism which is further informed by my various involvements in and with other communities. I am grateful to the various persons and theologies who have contributed in important and decisive ways to my theological development. I am convinced that communal and personal heartfelt worship and holistic witness will always be the primary concerns of Pentecostal life, and this is why I positioned the first and last chapter as I did. Living faithfully with the Social Trinity is living for the world as an alternative community and living compassionately with our fellow sisters and brothers in Christ. We worship because we know our Redeemer lives, and we witness so that others may come to experience the loving personal presence of the almighty God who can transform lives. Whether I have clearly presented and demonstrated a Pentecostal theology anchored in a common identity and based upon our primary central narrative convictions is left up to the readers.

Made in the USA
Middletown, DE
15 January 2016